£4.00

N2

DM

MAGIC AND WITCHCRAFT
OF THE BORDERS

Magic and Witchcraft of The Borders

MARION LOCHHEAD

with vignettes by James Hutcheson

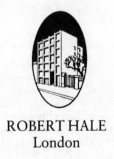

ROBERT HALE
London

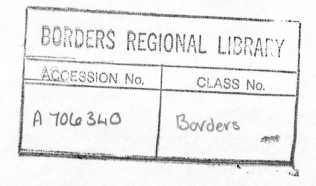
Photoset by Rowland Phototypesetting Ltd
Printed in Great Britain by
St Edmundsbury Press, Bury St Edmunds, Suffolk
Bound by Hunter & Foulis Ltd

Contents

6 *Contents*

Preface

The history of any country or region cannot be fully told without recourse to its legendary, magical and factual sources, to folk-tale, ballads and tradition, as well as to formal literature and printed records. In this kind of history the Scottish Borders are rich. Behind or within that region of fighters and reivers, farms, shepherds and fishermen lies the other country of enchantment, superstition, uncanny knowledge.

This book reports my adventures in the other country of the Borders. From the early nineteenth century there have been many travellers, many collectors, one of the greatest Scottish writers among them being Sir Walter Scott. Some of the tales here retold have needed that process, being, in their first vision, somewhat diffuse, over-elaborate in style. This is far from being an exhaustive collection, but it may be an introduction to a peculiar, rich and fascinating history.

Marion Lochhead

Introduction

The Borders are well named, for not only are they the debateable land between Scotland and England but they lie on the shadowy boundary between the land we know, of ordinary people and everyday life, and that other country where uncanny things happen, which is inhabited by those who are not of this earth or of human race, where mortals may be taken and whence those other folk may come, and not always with good purpose.

Every country, every region of that country, has its own magic. On the Borders it is largely witchcraft and wizardry, with tales of Elfhame and of the brownies, who are usually harmless and, if treated properly, positively helpful. The history and tradition of witchcraft are peculiarly strong, with more black than white about them. The inhuman powers are often satanic. Behind the black witches and warlocks is their master, the muckle de'il himself.

There is little or nothing about kings and queens, princes and princesses, who appear so often in Celtic legend as in French; little about giants, nothing about mermaids although we meet the kelpie, that unkind water-spirit.

The Mediterranean lands held, long after the coming of Christ, their memory of the old gods, the minor deities of field and wood and river, banished but not beyond recall. They departed slowly, the patron saints took over, but the difference was not always clear. There was an unbroken succession of tutelary divinities or semi-divinities. Was Pan overcome or was he accepted with compassion, kept in his place on condition of good conduct? The gentle spirits of stream and wood were not utterly condemned. And when St Francis came, he gave thanks for brother sun and sister moon, for brother fire and sister water who was so clean and serviceable and for mother earth herself.

There was no such tenderness in the Border tradition. Pan was of the tribe of Lucifer himself, if indeed he was known at all. He became Auld Hornie, the muckle de'il whose power was immense, for whose adherents there was one destination and that was hell. His followers were numerous and he gave them power, but he exacted payment and he was merciless. The failed witch or warlock was in most piteous case, beyond hope, beyond salvation.

There was, too, the middle region whose inhabitants were not of this earth, nor of heaven nor of hell: the elves, the fairies, the wee folk, known with propitiatory courtesy as 'the Good People' or 'the Good Neighbours'. They were not of the seed of Adam. Some held that they were among the fallen angels of less degree, those who had not been fierce or implacable in revolt against God, but disloyal all the same. There were innumerable half-forgotten deities of stream and field and wood, exiled but never far. They longed for mortals and loved to lure them away or, when they could, to steal an unchristened child or sometimes to take a human mother to nurse their babies. They were not utterly evil and cruel, yet neither were they steadfast in kindness or virtue; they were different, uncanny, with their own rules. And they were elusive, glamorous, taking 'glamour' as Sir Walter defined the word, which 'in the legends of Scottish superstition means the magic power of imposing on the eyesight of the spectators, so that the appearance of an object shall be totally different from the reality . . . it is a firm article of popular faith that no enchantment can subsist in a living stream, nay, if you can interpose a brook between you and witches, spectres, and even fiends, you are in perfect safety.'

Glamour affects time. Those who go into Elfhame may seem to themselves to stay only a day or a night, but when they return to earth they find their own generation has died, and there is none left who remembers them; or it may happen contrariwise: years of living in that other country may be found, by human measurement, to have lasted only for moments. This happened, as will be told, to one who was led away on an adventure by Michael Scot, one of the greatest of wizards.

There could, however, be equal measurement in time. Thomas the Rhymer was taken away, and

> Till seven years were come and gane,
> True Thomas on earth was never seen.

In *Tamlane*, too, Tam tells Janet, his faithful love, of his particular danger. Once in seven years those Other People 'maun pay a teind to hell', a stolen human if they can hold one, rather than one of themselves, and 'I'm feart it be mysel'.'

Elfhame, the place of illusion or glamour, lay apart from both heaven and hell as from earth. On their ride together the Queen of Elfhame shows Thomas two paths: one broad and fair, thronged with people – the way to hell, 'though some call it the way to heaven' – the other steep, rough and narrow – which is the road to paradise, 'though after it but few enquire'. Then they ride on to her kingdom and

> a' the blude that's shed on earth
> Rins through the streams o' that countrie.

There is little in Border poetry and legend about the road to heaven – with the lovely exception of *Kilmeny*, which tells of the girl who was taken away not by fairies or to any place of glamour but to the very borders of true paradise. She came back to this earth bringing peace to all creatures, but 'it wasna her hame and she couldna remain' – her place was with the angels and saints.

For most warlocks and witches earth was the place where they could work evil and fulfil their master's demands. They knew the broad way to hell, which for a time could be very pleasant until the end came. Black magic is strong in Border legend and was firmly believed by most people to exist and be active. There was, of course, a strong element also of human malice, cruel gossip, envy, jealousy, suspicion. A trickle of this gossip and surmise could swell to a flood of belief, and this malice could come within measuring distance of the black diabolic evil itself. The victim or suspect might be a bonny and healthy young lass full to the brim of sex appeal which, though not yet known by that name, was none the less present and potent. She might be an old wife, poor, solitary, neglected, full of bitter and envious thoughts, and these could be magnified and distorted into a diabolic vengeance. But there was undoubtedly an utter and inhuman evil. Witch-hunting could be damnably cruel, but the hunters could justify themselves by claiming that they were hunting the Devil himself in his followers. No one had the slightest doubt that there were real sorcerers, both men and women, who trafficked in an evil far deeper than any sin of the flesh – evil of the soul.

The Scot has a keen sense of sin, especially in others. He can smell it a mile off, he can even perceive it in himself, and this perception leads to the most perverse and dreadful form of pride – the exultance in his own evil nature, as James Hogg (1770–1835) has shown in *Confessions of a Justified Sinner* (1824), a work essentially of the Border mind and genius. As a rule, however, the Scot prefers to see sin in others and, having some power of imagination, to see it not merely as weakness of the flesh but as spiritual wickedness. To that may be added the dramatic nature of the Scottish imagination and creative instinct.

The man and woman who appear to know too much, who use their knowledge maliciously, who act malignantly, are easily made into agents of the Devil. The power of gossip is incalculable. A few sparks may set the wood on fire. That power might come to be recognized and discredited, but there was always the feeling that there's no smoke without fire, and some fires were kindled not by sparks of human mischief but by the hands of the Devil.

Walter Scott knew this too, and James Hogg, the Ettrick Shepherd, knew it and told it in tales like 'The Hunt of Eildon' and 'The Witches of Traquair'. They were both of the Borders, both with imagination quickened and fed by Border legend. They had spiritual heirs in Robert Louis Stevenson and John Buchan, the latter also of the Borders by inheritance and in upbringing. Stevenson's 'Thrawn Janet' is the very distillation of the uncanny and the evil, from the account of her appearance, and the attack on her by the women of the village to the final denunciation by the minister: 'Witch, beldame, devil . . . I charge you by the power of God begone – if you be dead, to the grave, if you be damned, to hell.' And when the black man, her master, her possessor, departed: 'There's little doubt but it was him that dwelled sae lang in Janet's body.'

Buchan wrote more than one tale of wizardry and diabolism: *The Dancing Floor*, *The Watcher on the Threshold* and the opening scene of *Prester John*. There is more than a touch of this quality too in *The Three Hostages*, when Richard Hannay realizes that Medina is an adversary possessed of no mere criminal power and malice. The climax of revelation of diabolism is reached in *Witch Wood*, with the minister's discovery of the black Mass, with the Devil himself as president, and a crowd of his apparently respectable parishioners as congregation.

How much of the belief in witchcraft and its practice came from the rejection of Our Lady and the saints and from the loss of liturgical worship? The Deity became remote and implacable; the Kirk subjected its members to mercilessly long sermons and extempore prayers almost as long; there was no action or response on the part of the congregation. The deep desire for worship, for liturgy, for a pattern of words and acts was perverted horribly into the dances and ceremonial ordained by Satan and his servants. Pan was banished or horribly transformed. Some faint memory of tutelary deities of the fields lay beneath the setting apart of 'the Gudeman's Croft' – 'Gudeman' being a propitiatory name for the evil one, just as 'the Good People' was for fairies. Scott knew about that: 'There must still be many alive who, in childhood, have been taught to look with wonder on knolls and patches of ground left uncultivated because, whenever a ploughshare entered the soil, the elemental spirits were supposed to testify their displeasure by storm and thunder.'

Scott was well named 'The Wizard of the North'. Those who gave him that title may hardly have realized the depth of his knowledge or the fascination held for him by magical and uncanny. Knowledge and imagination fused in him and were distilled into some of his poems and tales, into some of his notes on *The Lay of the Last Minstrel* (1805) and on his great collection *The Minstrelsy of the Scottish Border* (1802). His *Letters on Demonology and Witchcraft* came as near the end of his writing life as *The Minstrelsy* to the beginning. (They were addressed to Lockhart, and were published in 1830 by John Murray.) He wrote that: 'among much reading of my early days . . . I travelled a good deal in that twilight world of superstitious disquisitions. Many hours have I lost in examining old superstitions as well as more recent narratives of this character.' He spoke of: 'the credulity of our ancestors on such subjects . . . the almost universal belief in communication betwixt mortals and beings superior to themselves, and of a nature not to be comprehended by human organs . . . the general . . . universal belief of the inhabitants of this earth, in the existence of spirits separated from the encumbrances and incapacities of the body'. This belief was 'grounded on the consciousness of the divinity that speaks in our bosoms, and demonstrates . . . that there is within us a portion of the divine substance which is not subject to the law of death or dissolution, but which, when the body is no longer fit for its abode, shall seek it like a sentinel dismissed from his post'.

'Dismissed' is a harsh word, and the sentinel may join a company of the lost. Scott writes of the departed, of the company of haunting ghosts: '*Non omnis moriar* must infer the existence of many millions of spirits who have not been annihilated though they have become invisible to mortals. . . . These spirits . . . are not, it may be supposed, indifferent to the affairs of mortality, perhaps not incapable of influencing them. . . . To the multitude, the indubitable fact that so many millions exist around and even amongst us seems to support the belief that they are . . . by some means or other able to communicate with the world of humanity.'

On the human side, strong grief, or curiosity or great longing, could seek proof, visible and audible, of the survival of spirits who might be wandering in some shadowy world, which might lie close to hell. And the form of the departed might be assumed by servants of the Devil to mislead living men and women. Witchcraft is very ancient, but it can easily be believed that it developed greatly in Scotland after the Reformation, through rejection of the belief in purgatory, the place of purification, of pain willingly endured by the contrite and humble departed, a place of hope and of progress. Without belief in such a wholesome region, it became almost inevitable that the living should think of the departed as still in darkness, reaching out in longing, not for paradise, as would the souls in purgatory, but for the earth they knew, clutching at the living, possessive and demanding. On the one side there was a lust for knowledge, on the other a lust for power, that of the dead over the living, and that lust is more perilous than any strong and unlawful desires of the flesh. And here witchcraft found an entrance.

Witch-hunts were, as Scott found, much more common in Scotland than in England: 'While the divines of the Church of England possessed the upper hand in the kingdom, witchcraft, though trials and even condemnations for that offence occasionally occurred, did not create that epidemic terror which the very suspicion of the offence carried with it elsewhere. . . . It usually happened wherever the Calvinist interest became predominant in Britain, a general persecution of sorcerers and witches seemed to take place of consequence. Fearing and hating sorcery more than any other Protestants, connecting the ceremonies and usages with those of the detested Catholic Church, the Calvinists were more eager than other sects in searching after the traces of this crime, and, of course, unusually successful, as they might suppose, in making discoveries of guilt, and in pursuing it to the extirpation of the faggot. In a word . . . the number of the witches and their supposed dealings with Satan will increase or decrease according as such doings are accounted possible or improbable.'

Credulity can distort evidence, as Scott the man of law knew, and credulity could be strengthened by spite or bloodlust to become (in his word) an epidemic, even a mania, whereas: 'When the accusations are disbelieved, and dismissed as not worthy of attention, the crime becomes infrequent, ceases to occupy the public mind, and affords little trouble to the judges.'

The ferocity of witch-hunting in Scotland may have been intensified by the disappearance of popular festivals and holidays. In England the feasts of the Church's year were cheerfully kept: Christmas, Easter, Whit Sunday and other days and seasons. There were village fairs. The Presbyterian Scots, on the other hand, celebrated the New Year with even more drinking than usual, and Hallowe'en with age-old practices and ploys, not untinged by magic – but of holy days there was no pious remembrance unless among the Catholics and Episcopalians who prudently kept quiet about it. Witch-hunts gave the populace the stimulus which their forebears had found in fairs and sports. One cannot, of course, make rigid distinctions. It was an Episcopal king, James VI, who renewed and encouraged the attacks upon witches and warlocks and all their kind, and he could smell wizardry as keenly as he did tobacco. Of him Scott writes with delightful irony: 'Unfortunately, besides the more harmless freak of becoming a Prentice in the art of Poetry, by which words and numbers were the only sufferers, the monarch had composed a deep work upon Demonology, embracing in their fullest extent the most absurd and gross of the popular errors on this subject. He considered his crown and life as habitually aimed at by the sworn slaves of Satan.'

Hence came many persecutions, including that of 'the turbulent Francis Stewart, Earl of Bothwell', who made attempts upon the King's life and who had begun his career by consulting the weird sisters and soothsayers. A statute of the first year of James's reign described witchcraft 'by all the various modes and ceremonies in which, according to King James's fancy, that crime could be perpetrated, each of which was declared felony without benefit of clergy.... Men might now be punished for the practice of witchcraft as itself a crime.'

Scott adds a story of accusation of witchcraft which is comic rather than grim. A poultry-wife prospered greatly, both in rearing her own hens and in caring for and curing those of less successful keepers. Hence came jealousy, suspicion and gossip.

Once when she went to a farmer to buy grain for her fowls, she was rudely refused. His oats were all weighed and put into sacks for the market. The woman put a curse on him and his grain. Next morning, when his loaded cart was crossing the river, a wheel fell off, and some of the sacks toppled into the water – poetic justice indeed!

Another tale, told in one of those *Letters on Demonology and Witchcraft*, has more than a touch of the macabre. There was a weaver in North Berwick who lived happily with his wife and their three children, until the wife died on giving birth to a fourth child, leaving him in deep grief. After a year of widow-hood, though still mourning her, he decided to marry again, to have a helpmate for himself and a mother for his bairns. He chose wisely: a kind and comely woman whom he knew well. He was accepted and told the minister, asking him to read the banns on the following Sunday. That night he lay awake, his mind full of memories. At midnight a figure in white came into the room. She stood by his bed and told him that she was his lost wife, not dead but taken by the Other People, and that he could win her back. On a certain night he must go to the kirkyard with some neighbours and have the coffin disinterred and opened. Her body would rise and fly through the air. Then the strongest man and swiftest runner among them, whom she named, must follow and seize her, holding her fast. The spell would be lifted, and she would be restored to life and health and come back to husband and children.

The weaver did nothing at first. The figure appeared again next night, and again on the third. On that third night she lifted the baby from the cradle and gave it suck, letting a drop of milk fall on the floor. In the morning the bewildered man went to the minister with his story. The minister listened gravely and with compassion: 'That was not your wife: it was a phantom sent by the devil. Put from your mind all thought of what she said. Let me marry you today to the good woman you have chosen. I will dispense with the calling of the banns.'

The man took his advice, the bride was willing, and they were married that very day. The midnight visitant did not come again.

In *Guy Mannering*, Dirk Hatteraick, no estimable charac-

ter, accuses Meg Merrilees, the old gipsy wife, of witchcraft:
'The old devil's limb of a gipsy ... I'll meddle with her no
more – she's a witch of the fiend – a real devil's kind.' Meg is no
witch, but she can put a curse upon her adversaries: 'Ride your
ways, Laird of Ellangowan. Ride your ways, Godfrey Bertram.
This day have you quenched seven smoking hearths – see if the
fire in your ain parlour burn the blyther for that. Ye have riven
the thack of seven cotter houses – look if yer ain rooftree stand
the faster. . . . See that the hare does not couch on the hearthstane at Ellangowan.'

The hare on the bare hearth-stone is a common emblem of
desolation, as Thomas the Rhymer knew:

> The hare shall kittle on my hearthstand,
> But there'll ne'er be a Laird of Ercildoune again.

Scott, the Wizard of the North, has a close companion in
James Hogg, the Ettrick Shepherd, who inherited from his
mother and her forebears a wealth of lore and legend. It was
she who rebuked Scott for publishing *The Minstrelsy of the
Scottish Borders*, telling him that these poems were never
meant to be printed: 'Ye ha'e spoilt them a'thegither. They
were made for singing and no' for reading, and they're naither
richt spelt nor richt setten doun.' Scott took it meekly.

Her own father, known as 'Will o' Phaup', was the source of
one of the best and briefest of tales of the Other People.
Coming home late one night, he was met by three tiny boys
who begged 'up-putting for the nicht'. This he gladly promised. "Siccan shreds" as they would need, little room and little
food.

'Whaur dae ye come from?' he asked.

'From a place ye dinna ken.'

They asked him to give them a silver key which he had.

'In God's name whaur cam' ye from?', and there was no
reply. The tiny boys vanished at the speaking of the Holy
Name.

Hogg inherited much, and added to this heritage. He knew
the reality of evil, the malignity of the true witches and
warlocks, as in 'The Witches of Traquair'. It does not pay to be

a witch or a warlock. The Devil is a merciless master, as is shown in that tale and in 'The Hunt of Eildon'. He punished disobedience and failure with implacable cruelty. In 'The Hunt of Eildon', too, we find both kinds of witch-hunting: that which is justified, the hunting by the enchanted hounds of the women who are in league with the Devil against the King, and that which is malicious on the part of the hunters, when the poor innocent girl is taken, tried and condemned.

'The Brownie of the Black Haggs' is unique in plot but again is a plain warning of retribution – by what powers? – against malignity. Whence came that brownie? Hogg, too, gives us the tragic story of the phantom or haunting bride, of the doom which falls upon not only the treacherous lover but his innocent descendant.

Scott swept his mantle over John Buchan and Stevenson; Hogg touched them with his shepherd's crook. Buchan mentions the most elusive of wizards, not evil nor in servitude to Satan, a wandering warlock, lost and bewildered in the end: Merlin. The Arthurian legend is widespread from Cornwall and Glastonbury to the north, over the Border into the place of the last battle, to the Eildons where by one tradition Arthur sleeps with his knights, awaiting the summons to save Britain in her hour of desperate need. Buchan wrote in his preface to *Witchwood* that the parish 'lay in the shadow of a remnant of the wood of Caledon, that most ancient forest where once Merlin harped and Arthur summoned his men'. An old gamekeeper who had known it for fifty years, as had his father and grandfather before him, told the young Buchan that the trees of the wood had been 'first set by the Romans, others by auld Michael Scott himself', and it was 'a grand hidey-hole for beasts, and an unco bit for warlocks'.

Merlin comes into Border legend elusively and sadly, following his king. For Arthur, indeed, the Borders are the borderland between tradition or legend and history. He is said to have fought his last great battle against the heathen invaders at Coit Caledon, the wood of Caledon, and to have been slain – or taken hence – not to Avalon but to the Eildons.

For Merlin the end was harsh and bitter. He survived the battle and wandered about Tweedside, witless, mocked by the countryfolk, stoned to death, and lies buried by the Powsail Burn near Drumelzier. A kindlier, more Christian tradition has him meet St Kentigern or Mungo, Bishop of Strathclyde, from whom he learned the new faith and by whom he was baptized, so that he came to peace at the last. By an equally gentle legend, Thomas the Rhymer was after many years of human time released from Elfhame and, coming back to his own Tweedside, found refuge in a monastery.

There was a Thomas of Ercildoune, Thomas the Rhymer, given that title, as Scott tells us, for having composed 'a poetical romance on the subject of Tristram and Iseult, which is curious as the earliest specimen of English verse known to exist ... and like other men of talent of the period was suspected of magic'. The period was the reign of Alexander III, 1249–86. (The historical Thomas is the hero of Nigel Tranter's excellent novel *True Thomas*, where Michael Scot also appears and where the departure into Elfhame is simply and romantically an elopement with a human bride who wears a green riding cloak.)

In Scott's narrative Thomas in his first meeting with the Queen of Elfland descends from reverence (when he takes her at first for the Queen of Heaven) to bold wooing and is warned that if he persists he will become her slave. He is not deterred, and so begins his thraldom. Suddenly, 'the appearance of the beautiful lady is changed into that of the most hideous hag ... blighted and wasted as if by palsy ... her colour ... now a dun leaden hue,' and Thomas must follow her on a frightful journey, across rivers of blood, through a dark cavern, hearing the sound of a distant sea. The Queen regains her beauty. They pass a laden tree from which she forbids Thomas to pluck the fruit, for it is the fruit which tempted Eve and brought the fall of man. Then she shows him four roads: the steep and narrow way to heaven trodden by few, the broad and easy one to hell, much frequented, and that to Elfland which they are to follow; the fourth 'by yonder dark brake conducts to the milder place of pain from which prayer and mass may release offenders'.

They come within sight of a splendid castle: 'The lord of the castle is king of the country and I am his queen. But Thomas, I had rather be drawn with wild horses than he should know what hath passed between you and me. Therefore, when we enter yonder castle, observe strict silence and answer no question.'

It is the old fairy-tale prohibition: do not speak, do not ask, do not answer questions.

They enter the castle through the kitchen, where a great feast is being prepared – thirty deer are being roasted – then into the hall where the King welcomes his 'loving consort without censure or suspicion', where knights and ladies are dancing, and Thomas joins them.

Presently, as it appears to him, he is drawn aside by the Queen and bidden to depart and return to his own country. He has been seven years in Elfland, and it is urgent that he depart, for soon 'the fiend of hell' will come 'to demand his tribute', and a fine handsome man like Thomas will be his choice. So the Queen escorts him back to Huntly Bank, to the singing of birds and to a loving farewell. The Queen's parting gift is of 'the tongue that canna lee' and is not welcomed by Thomas, for it will 'make him unfit for church or fir market, for king's court or for lady's bower'. But it is laid upon him, and henceforth he is True Thomas.

So he returns to his own tower of Ercildoune, until one day when he is entertaining a company of guests with feast and harp and song. A hart and a hind come pacing through the forest, right up to the door of the tower. Thomas rises and carrying his harp leaves the tower and follows hart and hind through the forest beyond human sight or ken, back to Elfland.

One of his prophecies concerns himself:

> The hare shall kittle on my hearth-stane,
> And there will never be a Laird Learmont again.

Another foretells the death of Alexander III and that of his granddaughter, the Maid of Norway, who should have been Queen of Scots. And one tells of the Battle of Flodden where King James IV fell, but not in death, for legend tells that he was taken away to the Isle of Skye.

A more recent writer and scholar, the late William Croft Dickinson, has told in *The Eildon Tree* how two children of today meet Thomas under the tree and are taken by him into Elfland, where they are happy for a time and whence they return safely. In a sequel, *The Flag of the Isles*, they are taken with the King over the sea to Skye, and from that journey in time and space they come safely home.

Thomas the Rhymer, True Thomas, is immortal. He put his spell upon a Victorian novelist who is not usually credited with a knowledge of that other country: Dinah Maria Craik (1826 –87), born Mulock in Stoke-on-Trent where her father was a Nonconformist minister. From girlhood she was aware of her vocation as writer. In 1846 she came to London, where she met two men who helped her to follow that vocation: Daniel Macmillan, who published her books, and Edward Mudie, who bought them in quantities for his lending library. In 1864 she married George Craik, a partner in Macmillan's.

Her *John Halifax, Gentleman* appeared in 1857 and was popular for decades to come, given to young Victorians and Edwardians as a Sunday School prize, approved Sunday reading even in strict households. It is a good story, an excellent period piece and, like all its author's work, highly professional.

That record sounds very matter-of-fact, completely Victorian. But there was another self in her, open to enchantment, able to convey it. In 1863 she published a delightful volume of old tales retold, *The Fairy Book*, and before that, in 1852, had come *Alice Learmont*, which tells how a descendant of Thomas the Rhymer was taken away to that other country where she met her ancestor and whence she came back to her own home and her mother.

The magic of the Borders has compelled a succession of writers, from a great genius to patient collectors, to make and share their discovery of that other country. There is glamour in it, there is true love, there is more than a glisk of evil. There was real witchcraft as well as persecution of pitiful old women. There was the passion for forbidden power and knowledge. The spell of elfdom recurs; the way between that realm and human habitation is often open.

There are warlocks and mages, there is tragedy and some comedy, but perhaps not very much holiness. The saints would not appear to have frequented the Borders.

Witches and Warlocks

Michael Scot, the Wizard

Michael Scot was truly a scholar, one of the wandering scholars of the Middle Ages who meandered across Europe, studying in the universities of France, Italy and Spain. Their learning was so wide and profound as to overawe the unlettered multitude, and from awe to belief in their wizardry was a step over a dimly marked line. The legend of magical powers in Michael was moreover a form of self-defence by the common people, with a tinge of mockery, a form even of leg-pull.

A Victorian scholar and cleric, James Wood Brown, sympathetically brought together both elements, the scholarship and the legendary wizardry, in a life of Michael Scot which would undoubtedly have delighted his namesake the Wizard of the North, Sir Walter. His source was a Life by a sixteenth-century scholar and was part of a treatise on mathematics. The writer, Bernardino Baldi, was Abbot of Guastallo. Of his work only two copies existed, both in private possession, kept under seal. But in 1707 a *Chronicade Mathematica*, an *Epitome of Lives*, was printed, and this was discovered and used by Wood Brown, to good effect, to our entertainment as well as instruction. He calls Michael 'a judicial astrologer' and describes his career from his leaving the Borders to its climax in the service of the Emperor Frederick at his court in Sicily.

There is an evocative description of the Border country the wizard knew, of forests changing slowly to pasture-land, a country haunted by magic: 'The deep woods were not only scenes of labour . . . they were homes of mystery in which the young imagination loved to dwell, peopling them with half-human shapes more graceful than their stateliest trees, and half-brutal monsters, more terrible than the fiercest wolf and bear. The distant sun and stars . . . were an unexplored scene of wonder, which patient and brooding thought alone could reach and interpret.'

Scholars migrated like swallows or wild geese in winter to the warmth of the south. Michael's first flight was to Oxford, then to Paris and to Bologna. He was a Master of Arts (and some believed these to include the black art of magic). Then came the climax of his true career – his appointment to the household of Frederick II, King of Sicily and Emperor of Germany (born 1194, died 1250). Much of his time was thereafter spent in Palermo, a far cry from the dark woods and hills of the Borders. Europe is the setting for Michael the scholar, the Borders for Michael the Wizard: a double life created by legend.

He has an affinity in modern times with the late M. R. James, scholar, antiquary, expert in medieval manuscripts, Provost of Eton and of King's College, Cambridge, and author of some of the most convincing and blood-chilling ghost stories ever told. There may yet be an M. R. James legend of wizardry, and among the books which should have been written for our delight and our terror is a *Life of Michael Scot* by that spiritual kinsman of our own day.

Michael studied at one time in Spain, at Toledo, that meeting-place of two cultures and two faiths, the Christian and the Mohammedan-Moorish-Arabic. Here too began the discovery of revival of Aristotelianism, the renaissance of pure scholarship. Michael was a notable Aristotelian, and this phase of his life seems like an image of scholarly retreat at Oxford or Cambridge. He tasted the very essence and distillation of learning. He translated Averroës of Cordoba, he wrote treatises on astronomy and on alchemy, he was a scientist, a philosopher, a classicist, a theologian and also a courtier, ranking high in the service of the King-Emperor Frederick.

It is all rather overwhelming, and the growth of the legend of the wizard on his own Tweedside is a form of self-defence by the common folk. It is itself at once magic, sometimes with a tinge of the diabolic, and comical. Comedy, after all, is a strong defence against magic, a good weapon.

Most of the tales of his ploys belong to the Borders, but one is from his days at court in Sicily. The young Emperor Frederick, newly (in 1220) crowned in Rome, gave a banquet to celebrate in his palace of Palermo. The guests were gathered in the great hall, the pages carrying basins of rose-water and fine linen towels for the washing of hands. Michael suddenly appeared with a companion, both dressed in Eastern robes. He offered to perform some magic for the entertainment of the company while they awaited dinner. Frederick begged for rain, for the weather was oppressively hot and dry. The wizard spoke the word, and a storm of rain descended; he spoke again and the rain ceased, leaving the earth and air cool and fresh. The Emperor bade Michael choose his reward for this boon.

'Grant me, sir, a champion to defend my comrade and myself against our enemies.'

'Choose now your champion,' said Frederick, and the wizard chose the young Baron Ulfo, who gladly accepted the adventure.

They left Palermo, sailing in two galleys with a company summoned by Michael, and sailed westward into strange seas, to a strange and lovely land where the people welcomed them, for they were under the rule of a tyrant king. A host of these people joined the company of Michael and his companion and Ulfo, who took command. His army, now a great one, defeated that of the tyrant, who was killed. The people, in joy and gratitude, implored Ulfo to take the kingdom. The cruel King had left a daughter who was lovely and gentle and good, loved and pitied by the people. (It happens often in fairy tale that a tyrant, a giant, even an ogre, somehow has a daughter of great gentleness and beauty who helps the hero.) Baron Ulfo fell deeply in love with her, and she with him. They were crowned king and queen of the land and lived and reigned together happily and benevolently for twenty years. They had children worthy of them, and the kingdom prospered before Michael and his companion departed.

Then they returned and summoned Ulfo to go with them

again. He obeyed, thinking this another adventure from which
he would return to his kingdom, to his beloved Queen and
their family. They sailed in a galley which brought them to
Sicily; they came to Palermo and into the banqueting hall of
the castle. All the guests were there, just as they had been, the
pages leaving the hall after carrying round the basins of
rose-water and the fine linen towels for the washing of hands.
Time had not passed or changed here, as it had in Ulfo's
kingdom. Michael and his companion departed again while
Ulfo remained. For him there was no return to his own
kingdom; for the rest of his life he mourned his lost love, his
most beautiful Queen and the children. Twenty years had
vanished like a dream.

And *there* is the ancient, recurring motif of illusion, of
glamour. Sir Walter Scott knew all about this and described it
in *The Lay of the Last Minstrel*. Glamour makes

> The cobwebs on a dungeon wall
> Seem tapestry in lordly hall;
> A nutshell seem a golden barge,
> A sheiling seem a palace large,
> And youth seem age, and age seem youth, –
> All was delusion, naught was truth.

He adds a note: '*Glamour*, in the legends of Scottish superstition, means the magic power of imposing on the eyes of the
spectators, so that the appearance of an object shall be totally
different from the reality.'

There is the timelessness of Elfhame. A man may spend what
seems to him a night in the fairy hill and, coming out in the
morning, return to his own home and place but find that scores
of years have passed; or he may seem to live for years in that
other place, to marry and have children, then to come back and
find that no time has passed, his absence has not been noticed,
all is as it was – except for the heartache and longing.

Michael in his real life in Italy took holy orders. He lived for
a time in the warmth of papal approval. Pope Honorius II
commended him to Stephen Langton, Archbishop of Canter-

bury. He was offered the see of Cashel in Ireland but declined it, not having the Gaelic, the language of the people. Pope Gregory IX (successor to Honorius) also favoured him, but no preferment in Britain came his way.

Like his fellow Borderer Thomas the Rhymer, Michael made prophecies. One foretold the manner of death of the Emperor Frederick: that he would die at the gates of a town named after the goddess Flora. Thereafter Frederick avoided the city of Florence. But in 1250, when on campaign, he fell ill – in the town of Fiorentino in Apulia. He lay in a room in the castle tower. His bed stood by a wall, newly built to fill the old gateway of the tower, and in that wall there were still the iron staples of the gate. When he heard that, Frederick made no effort toward recovery. The prophecy must be fulfilled, the will of God obeyed, his doom accepted.

The other prophecy foretold Michael's own death – from a stone falling upon his head. He even foretold the weight of the stone. And so it came about. As he knelt in prayer at Mass, head uncovered and bowed, he was struck by a stone shaken loose from the church tower by the clang of the bell.

His legend long outlived him. *Credo quia impossibile*; it is too good to be disbelieved. He is truly of the company of the *vates*, along with Virgil and Thomas the Rhymer.

His cleaving of the Eildon Hills is not the only magic wrought there. Who knows who sleeps within those hills? The Borders have their own account of the departure of Arthur, of his sleeping with his chosen knights within that hillside, and not in some far southern Avalon.

Scott has a tale of a countryman in Roxburghshire who sold a horse to an old man whom he had never seen before and who said to him: 'Meet me at midnight at the Lucken How in Eildon, and there I will pay you.'

Buyer and seller duly kept the tryst, and payment was made, in antique coin.

'Will you visit my dwelling?' asked the old man. The countryman accepted and followed his guide into the hill, to find himself in a great stable where rows of horses stood, saddled and bridled, each carrying his rider.

'They will waken for Shirramuir, and ride then,' said the old man. He pointed to a horn hung on the wall beside a sheathed sword. 'They will waken at the sound of the horn.'

The countryman, greatly daring, took down the horn and blew a blast. The horses awoke, stirred and pawed the ground. Their riders stirred but did not waken. The countryman heard the sound of their armour and weapons.

A voice cried: 'Woe to him who does not unsheath the sword before he has blown the horn.'

The man dropped the horn. He found himself back on the hillside – how he had been brought there again, and by whom, he could not tell. He could see no entrance into the hillside. And he had the sense not to try to find any or seek another adventure.

Michael served his own monarch, the King of Scots, as faithfully as he had served the Emperor, and with a touch of magic power. He was sent once on a mission to the King of France, demanding redress and restoration of booty taken by some French pirates. The wizard-diplomat summoned his familiar or demon, pronounced a spell which turned him into a horse, mounted and rode through the air to Paris. The French King was reluctant to make or promise any payment. Michael begged him to delay his decision until the horse had struck the ground with his hoof three times. At the first stroke all the bells of Paris jangled. At the second, three of the palace towers fell to the ground. There was no third stroke of the hoof. The French King granted all that his royal cousin of Scotland demanded.

If there is irony in that tale, there is some rough comedy in the account of his dealing with the Witch of Fauldshope. He was staying at Oakwood Tower nearby and heard of her ongoings and went to visit her, to order her to give up those practices. She denied, smooth-tongued, all knowledge or use of witchcraft; but when he laid his staff for a moment on the table, she seized it, touched him, uttered a spell – and the great wizard became a hare.

He fled, pursued by his own hounds, and only just managed to reach a hiding-place. There he uttered a counter-spell which restored him to his true shape. He recovered his staff, but he did not wholly recover his confidence. He was filled with a desire for revenge, though not untinged with respect for the witch-woman. She had won the first trick. She must win no more.

For most of her time she was a respectable woman, wife of a farmer. She was known to be a very good baker. Michael sent his servant to her, asking for some loaves. As he had expected, she refused. He had given his servant a scroll to use if this occurred. The man, unobserved by the witch-wife, busy about her work, stuck the scroll on the outside of the door. It was inscribed with words and symbols of power and with this rhyme:

> Maister Michael Scot's man
> Socht bried and gat nane.

The servant went back to his master, and with one or two others they went to stand on a hill overlooking the cottage.

It was harvest time and the witch-wife was making porridge for the harvesters' dinner. But as soon as the wizard's servant departed, leaving the scroll on the door, she began running round and round the kitchen, uttering the words of the rhyme.

The wizard and his companions looked down, and laughed, and waited. Presently the harvesters came back from the fields, hungry for their porridge. As soon as they entered the house – they took no time to look at the scroll on the door – they too began to run round and round the kitchen after the woman, uttering the rhyme. They ran till they nearly dropped with exhaustion.

Then the woman's husband came. He had begun to suspect some trickery when his men did not come back.

He saw the scroll on the door, so he had the sense not to enter but looked through the window. There he saw the wild race of his wife and his men, round and round the kitchen, the woman gasping and stumbling on the verge of exhaustion. He looked at the mad whirling dance, then he turned and looked up the hill and saw Michael.

He walked up, bowed to the wizard and humbly begged release for those unhappy runners. Michael granted his plea. He bade the man return to the cottage, remove the scroll from the door and enter the house backward. The man obeyed; the wild dance ceased and the poor wife collapsed, nearly dead. She lay long in her bed, weak and ill. There was no more witchery from her.

Michael Scot went once from Scotland on a special embassy to the Pope. For the ordering of the calendar, the Church's year, it is necessary to know the date of Ash Wednesday, when Lent or Shrovetide begins. On that depends the date of Easter, of the Ascension and of Whit Sunday. So every year, early in the spring, a man of learning and distinction was sent to ask the Holy Father the date of Ash Wednesday.

Michael Scot had been appointed but, being full of affairs, dealings with witches no doubt among them, he put off his departure, perhaps forgot, until he realized that Candlemas was over and Shrovetide must be near. So he summoned a fairy horse.

'How fast can you ride?' he asked.

'As fast as the wind.'

'That is not fast enough.'

He summoned another horse: 'How fast can you ride?'

'So fast that I outstrip the wind that blows behind me, and overtake the wind that blows before me.'

'Neither is that fast enough.'

He summoned a third horse: 'What is your speed?'

'Swifter than the black blast of March.'

'That is swift, but not swift enough.'

A fourth horse was summoned: 'What is your speed?'

'I am as swift as the thought of a girl between her two lovers.'

'That is speed enough,' the wizard declared. He mounted and rode the horse over land and sea.

As they rode, the horse asked: 'What do the women of Scotland say when they smoor the fire at night?'

'Ride on, you, in your master's name, and ask no questions.'

'A blessing on you, but a curse on whoever gave you that answer.'

They rode on swiftly, then the fairy horse asked: 'What do the women of Scotland say when they put a child to sleep in the cradle, and hold a baby to their breast?'

'Ride on, you, in your master's name, and let the women of Scotland sleep in peace.'

'A blessing on you, but a curse on the woman who first put a finger in your mouth.'

When they came to Rome, in the early morning, Michael alighted by the Pope's palace and sent word to His Holiness that he had come to ask the date of Shrovetide. The Pope had him brought to the hall of audience.

'Whence come you?' asked the Pope.

'From the faithful in Scotland who desire to know the date of Ash Wednesday, lest Shrovetide go away from us.'

'My blessing upon the faithful in Scotland, but you come late,' said His Holiness.

'Then I have no time to lose,' said Michael.

'You have ridden high?'

'Neither high nor low, but straight ahead.'

'There is snow on your bonnet.'

'That is the snow of Scotland, Your Holiness.'

'What proof can you give me of that or of your having come from Scotland?'

'I can tell you this, Holy Father, that the shoe on your right foot is not your own shoe.'

The Pope looked down, and there on his right foot was a woman's shoe.

'Your request is granted,' he told the wizard, and he told him the date of Ash Wednesday and Shrovetide. He told him too how he knew, from the rising and waxing of the moon, when that day would fall from year to year. No other messenger had been given this knowledge; they had been told only the date of the coming Shrovetide. And that special knowledge Michael kept to himself.

Sources:
Sir Walter Scott, *The Lay of the Last Minstrel*
James Wood Brown, *Life and Legend of Michael Scot*
Sir George Douglas, *Enquiry into the Scottish Fairy and Folk Tales*

Magic, Mischief and Devilry

The Borders have their own magic, akin to that of the Celtic regions in the Highlands, in Ireland, Wales and Brittany, but with a difference. There is less about kings and princesses, about giants and about the little people who live in their raths or hills. There is more about witches and warlocks, especially the former, for the female is usually deadlier than the male; there is a good deal about brownies and bogles, and a certain amount about the Devil himself, whom the Scots regard with a mixture of sound fear and awareness of his power, and a no less wholesome hint of mockery and humour: Auld Nick, Auld Hornie, Auld Cloutie or Clovenhoof.

There was a field near Berwick known as Cloutie's Croft or the Gudeman's Field which was left untended, unsown, unmown. There is holy ground, there is common earth, there is unholy ground, and wise folk know the difference.

We are told of one old woman who spoke of Auld Cloutie with something approaching charity. She heard no evil, saw no evil, spoke no evil – not so much as a whisper of gossip and scandal – which made her a dull neighbour in the opinion of some folk.

'Ach, wumman,' declared an exasperated neighbour, 'I believe ye'd ha'e a gude word to say aboot the de'il himself!'

'Ach, weel, he's an eydent body,' was the reply.

He is not, the Lord be thanked, omnipotent, nor is he

armoured against all thrusts – as one good minister knew. This cleric was riding home late one night from a meeting of the presbytery. His way led across desolate moorland. Suddenly he heard a laugh, and his horse also heard it, stumbled and threw his rider. The laugh was repeated, louder and more raucous than before. Shaken but unhurt, the minister pulled himself up, remounted and rode on, calling out: 'Aye, Satan, I've ta'en a dunt and ye may laugh. But when I fa', I can rise again. Ye fell aince – but ye ha'e ne'er risen again.' There was no more laughter but a deep horrible groan, and the minister rode safely home.

The Devil takes many forms: that of an old man, or in some accounts a young, handsome fellow; that of a cat, the commonest familiar among witches, of a great black dog, of a goat, of a ram with long horns, of a bull, of a black crow; but never that of a lamb or a dove, for the one is blessed by the Lamb of God, and the Holy Spirit broods with dove-wings over redeemed mankind.

In his human form, which could be ordinary enough, neither aged and fearsome nor young and handsome, he is said to have tried many trades and succeeded in none, which must be a comfort to decent good tradesmen and craftsmen. When he tried weaving, he pricked his fingers so sorely with the pins that he gave up; as a tailor he cut everything wrong and was dismissed by his master; as a shoemaker he could not make a shoe to fit any foot and was again thrown out. He went as apprentice to a blacksmith but drove the nails into his own hand instead of the horse's hoof. As a would-be carpenter he fell over the logs which he was about to saw, and he cut himself with the saw and with every tool he took up. (This was surely the last trade he should have tried, for the patron of carpenters is that douce, strong, kindly man St Joseph, who taught his craft to Our Lord himself.)

Finally he took to making up drinking songs, and in this he had some luck, for his songs are still sung in pubs and inns about the countryside; nor is the audience hyper-critical.

Witches appear frequently in Border lore. Some of them were intimate with their master Auld Nick; some were apprentice hands, up to all the mischief they could do. There was a canny man called Ronaldson in the village of Bowden who found a good way to deal with them. Early one morning he was standing with his foot on a low dyke, tying his garter. Suddenly he heard some not very agreeable laughter, although there was no one within sight. A rope of straw was pulled between his legs, and suddenly he was lifted and carried off.

He was set down for a moment by a burn at the foot of one of the Eildons and again heard that mocking laugh. Then he was lifted again and carried on a bit further, to a ford known as the brig o' stanes. Here again he was set down and again he heard the laughter, but this time, with all his wits about him and a bit of piety, he called out: 'In the name of the Lord ye'll get me nae further.' The rope broke, and he found himself free. 'We've lost the cuif,' cried a voice, but he was no cuif (fool), and in next to no time he was safely home.

These witches might not have done him any great harm, but they would certainly have done him no good.

Another encounter was between a tailor's apprentice and a farmer's wife, at Deloraine. She was a good wife to her man, whatever she may have been up to in her own time, and she engaged the village tailor to come with his men, for the day, and make the farmer a new coat and new breeks.

'Come as early as ye can,' she told them, and they came for breakfast and were given porridge and milk. There was no stinting of the porridge, but the large milk jug was soon emptied. The wife took up the jug and went out to the kitchen. The tailor's youngest apprentice, who was not particularly given to minding his own business, followed her quietly. But she did not go to the dairy. She went to the byre, though it was long past milking time. So the lad followed and hid behind the door. The wife tirled a pin in the wall and held the jug beneath it, and a stream of milk flowed into it. When the jug was full, she tirled the pin the other way, and the flow of milk stopped. The lad ran back to the kitchen, the woman came in with the full jug, and soon everyone had had enough and was ready to start work.

The farmer went to his fields, his wife went about her work, and the tailors settled down to theirs. Towards noon one of them said: 'This is dreich wark. I'd like fine to ha'e a drink o' the milk the mistress gi'ed us wi' oor parritch. It was fine and creamy.'

'It was that,' agreed the master tailor, 'and I'd relish a draught mysel.''

The lad smiled to himself and slipped out – he was nearest the door and no one noticed him go. He found the bowl on a shelf, slipped out to the byre, tirled the pin and filled the bowl with the milk that flowed out. That was fine – but he could not turn the pin back again and had to leave the stream of milk flowing.

'It'll stop itsel',' he thought, and went back with the full bowl.

'I've brocht some milk,' he announced, and they all had a good drink.

'That was fine.' 'Aye, that will keep me going.' 'It's gude milk here,' they said. Then the farmer's wife came in, looking as grim and angry as any of them had seen a woman look.

'What ha'e ye dune, ye graceless loons? Wha brocht that milk? Ye've drawn the milk frae every coo in every farm between the head of Yarrow and the foot! Could ye no' ha'e asked for it, civil-like?'

The lad cowered down, the others looked ashamed. They went on with their work and were given their dinner, a good dinner of kale and champit tatties, plenty of both, and bannocks forbye, but there was not a drop of milk for the rest of the day. What the master and the other men said to that lad who thought himself so clever has not been recorded, but no doubt it was pungent. 'Mind your own business' is a good rule.

That goodwife did no harm – she does not even appear to have put any sort of spell upon the lad, such as making him squint or have warts on hands and face. The blacksmith's wife of Yarrowfoot was another type, and the lad who dealt with her had plenty of courage and resourcefulness. He and his younger brother were apprenticed to the blacksmith, a decent man. They were good lads, strong workers, learning their craft; healthy too, and sturdily built as a smith needs to be. So it was strange and distressing when the younger one began to dwindle and dwine, losing his appetite and strength. His brother, who was concerned, kept asking him what ailed him, and at last the poor boy told his tale.

'It's the mistress,' he said. 'She comes to the bedside at night, drags me oot, puts a bridle over my heid and turns me into a horse. Then she rides oot to the moors or some ither uncanny place and meets ithers like her, and they dance and carry on. It's no canny, it's fearsome. Then she rides me hame, rides me hard, tak's aff the bridle, and I can barely crawl back into bed and ha'e nae sleep afore it's time to get up. I canna sleep, I canna eat, I canna wark, I canna get the foul sights oot o' my mind.'

'We'll see to that,' declared his brother. 'Let's change places in the bed. You sleep in my place next the wa'; I'll tak' the outside.'

That was done. The younger brother, utterly weary, fair forfochen, fell asleep. The elder lay awake till midnight. The woman came in carrying a bridle. She dragged him up, threw the bridle over his head – and there stood a fine hunting horse. The woman mounted, touched him with her whip and rode off furiously. The tryst, this time, was in the wine cellar of a mansion nearby. The witch left her horse in the stable. He began rubbing his head on the wall, shaking it, rubbing it, until the bridle fell off and at once he was himself again. He picked up the bridle and stood behind the door.

'I'll sort ye, my wumman,' he muttered to himself and waited.

The Devil is a cunning as well as an eydent chiel – an industrious chap, and his followers are cunning too. But like their master, these people have a stupid streak in them: they think highly of themselves, poorly of others, and it is a mistake to underestimate your opponent. After a while the witch came back to the stable, with no idea at all of finding any trouble. The horse, which she had thought such a stupid lad, would be there, bridled and ready. Besides, she was a bit fuddled, having drunk well of the laird's excellent wine – and what he said when he discovered the drain made by his uninvited guests is not known but can be imagined if you have a good vocabulary. Well, in came the witch, and the lad was ready for her; he dropped the bridle over her head, and there stood a grey mare.

He mounted and rode her off furiously: up and down a newly ploughed field, across a moor, up a hill and down again, so fast that she dropped a shoe from each forefoot. Then he rode her back to her man's own smithy, shod her, took off the bridle and let her go. She crawled into the house, into her room and into bed beside her sleeping husband, fair forfochen.

The lad went to his own bed, beside his sleeping brother, slept for an hour or two, woke and told his brother all about it. They both rose and got ready for the day's work. Their master also awoke and got up; he tried to rouse his wife, who whimpered and cried, 'I'm no' weel. I canna rise. I ha'e sair pains.'

The good man went at once for the doctor, who came back with him, looked at the woman and pronounced her ill. 'Let's feel your pulse,' he said, but she hid her hands under the blanket.

'Let the doctor see yer haun's,' her husband told her, and he dragged them out. To each palm was nailed a horseshoe.

The doctor, horrified, went to the minister, and then on to Selkirk to report to the sheriff, so that the woman was brought to trial. The two apprentices were called as witnesses. The woman was found guilty of witchcraft and burned to death.

They were lucky, those lads; the younger regained his strength. No more is told of the witch's husband, whether he lived in the blackness of shame or got over it and went on with his life and his craft, and maybe found another wife, a decent one.

Whether those witches of Bowden who carried off young Ronaldson would have done him dire harm we do not know. He too was lucky, thanks to his own resourcefulness. So was the miller of Holdean in Berwickshire. He had been grinding and drying a crop of oats and, tired after the day's work, fell asleep in the barn above the kiln. He was awakened by loud, muddled voices as of a crowd, by their laughter and by the thud of feet. Pulling himself to the edge of the kiln, he looked down and saw a crowd of legs and great hairy feet trampling the warm ashes below. He could not make out what the voices were saying, but he guessed they meant no good. He took up his heavy wooden mell (hammer) and threw it down among the feet, calling out:

'What think ye o' my muckle mell? That'll gar thae muckle feet o' yours dance anither jig.'

There was silence, then a confusion of voices and yells of laughter. A huddle of folk came out, a gey queer lot to look at. As they departed they sang:

> Mount and fly for Rhymer's Tower!
> Ha, ha, ha, ha, ha!
> The pawky miller has beguiled us,
> Or we'd ha'e stown his luck for seven years to come!
> An' muckle watter wad ha'e run
> While the miller slept!

Source:
William Henderson, *Notes on the Folklore of the Northern Counties of England and the Borders*

The Hunt of Eildon

Gale, the young shepherd, lay on the slope of one of the Eildon Hills, talking to his dog, Trimmy, a wise creature, watchful and gentle.

'I hope the King will not hunt today, Trimmy, my lass, so that you and I can look after the lambs in peace.'

Gale spoke well, as often in book-English as in Scots, for he had had some schooling from the monks of Melrose Abbey.

'Why is it, Trimmy, that you shrink from the King's two white hounds? They are noble beasts, the swiftest and most graceful I have seen, and they have shown no ill will to you or to our flocks. Yet whenever they appear, you tremble and run away with your tail between your legs. I have never seen you flee from any other hounds, or from any beast or man. What is it, Trimmy, my lass? What ails you?'

Trimmy answered with a wag of her tail, licked Gale's hand and lay peacefully beside him. Up the hillside came Gale's fellow-shepherd Croudy, with his dog, Mumps, a rough, shaggy beast like his master, but a good sheepdog and faithful. Croudy, like Gale, was talking to his dog.

'It's a gey queer business, Mumps, my man. If the maister were to say to me: "That doug Mumps is a stupid beast" – that wad be a lee; I ken better. And if I were to tell the maister that I had heard thae bonny white hounds o' the King, Mooly and Scratch, talkin' thegither like humans, he'd say it was a lee, a muckle lee. But it is the truth. I ha'e heard them, and it's no' canny, Mumps, my man.'

Mumps wagged his tail in agreement. Croudy came up to Gale, and the two spoke briefly to each other, then each went off on his separate way with his dog.

A roe deer started up, running swiftly.

'So the hunt is up,' Gale said to himself and to Trimmy. 'The King will be riding up from the abbey with his company and those bonny white hounds.'

The King had indeed just left the abbey where he was staying and was riding towards the hill. He was intensely proud of his two beautiful swift hounds. Last night he had made a bet with Lord Home and Lord Belhaven that they would take and kill a deer started on the hill before the hunt rode out from the abbey. The bet was seven steers, seven palfreys, seven hounds and seven gold rings.

'And I'd wager more than that: I'd wager half my kingdom on these hounds.'

The two lords had bowed and accepted the wager. But they had come up the hill, started a roe deer and waited two or three minutes before blowing the horn to warn the King. The hunt came streaming up the hill, the graceful white hounds running by the King's horse. They snuffed the ground, trying to pick up the scent, at first apparently without luck. The two lords looked slyly at each other and laughed. Then suddenly the hounds picked up the scent and were off, as swiftly as the wind; they were like two white swans in flight; the swiftest horse could not come up with them.

'There they go, Trimmy,' said Gale. But Trimmy was not there. She was running away from the hunt, running back towards Eildon Hall in a panic that her master could not understand.

When the King and his company caught up with Mooly and Scratch, they found them standing over the body of a roe deer, newly killed. As the riders dismounted, an old man, tall and dignified, grey-headed and venerable, stood before the King. No one had seen him come, nor did anyone know where he had come from. The two lords, disconcerted, began to mutter that this might not be the deer that had been started, for no one had seen the kill.

'My lord king,' asked the old man, 'have you or anyone ever

seen these hounds kill a deer? Is it not strange that more than one deer has been found, newly slain with the hounds standing over the body, yet none has witnessed the killing?'

The King was silent. It was true that he had never seen the actual kill, although the hunt had come up very quickly with the hounds.

'Where did you get these hounds, from whom and when?' the old man went on. 'Was it not about the time when the daughters of Roslin, the ladies Clara and Ellen, disappeared?' The King stared at him with a troubled look, of fear and amazement. 'Did you buy or borrow them?'

'Neither,' said the King. 'I was given them for a token.'

'By whom?'

Then the King looked at his tormentor in anger. 'Who are you who dare thus question your king? Who is this?' he turned to his lords. 'Do you know him, my Lord Home?'

'I do – and yet I am not sure. I have surely seen him, but I cannot recall his name, or where I met him. He must be the Devil himself', and Lord Home laughed uneasily. They all turned to look again at the old man, but he was no longer there. None had seen him go, as none had seen him come. He had vanished like a mist or a shadow, leaving no trace. The King, greatly perturbed, touched his rosary and made the sign of the cross to invoke Our Lady. The hunt rode back to the abbey, leaving the deer where it lay.

Gale found his flock scattered and went quietly about the work of bringing them together. Trimmy came back with her tail between legs, looking abashed. Gale spoke gently: 'So here you are, Trimmy lass. What ailed you? But I don't blame you, there's uncanny business about.' Trimmy wagged her tail, and they worked together all day as usual.

Later Gale went to find Croudy, who was lying in a grassy hollow, near his flock, talking to himself and to Mumps.

'Did Mumps run from the King's hounds too?' asked Gale.

'He did that, and sma' wonder. Thae beasts are no' canny. Listen noo, Gale, to what I ha'e to tell. Yesterday when I heard the horn, I climbed up into a tree, right up to the tapmost branches that hid me, to see the hunt. There was no deer, but a bonny leddy cam' rinnin', rinnin' fast as if in fear, aye luikin' back. She ran close to the tree. Then the two white hounds cam' rinnin' efter her, and they sprang on her and brocht her doun. She cried oot and lay still. The hounds stood owre her and said ane to t'ither:

'"Wha is it this time?"

'"It's the Leddy Grizel. I ken her by her gowden rings."

'"That mak's twenty," said the first. "Oor wark's near dune, dear sister."

'"But we have still to save the King," said t'ither. "The attack on his life will be made tonight."

'Then they rolled themsel's on the body o' the leddy, and when they rose, there was nae leddy there but a deid deer. Syne the King and his company cam' ridin' up, and fine and pleased they were to see that bonny beast. A' this time I lay quakin' in the branches, for fear I'd be seen. The hunt rade awa'. I cam' doun. Mumps was gane but he cam' back. An' noo there's been anither deer killed, and wha that may ha'e been is a dreid question.'

'Strange indeed,' said Gale soberly. Had he heard that tale the day before, he might have laughed at Croudy, but now . . . 'Are you sure you didn't dream it all?' He would have been glad to think this was so.

'Dreamed it?' said Croudy angrily. 'Sleep and dream in the Eildon tree? No' likely. I've tel't ye what I saw wi' my ain eyes and heard wi' my ears; I was tellin' honest Mumps aboot it this verra mornin'.'

'I don't like it,' Gale told him gravely. 'We had better make this known at the abbey. These hounds, beautiful and swift as they are, are a menace and may well be possessed. But first let us tell Pery about it; she is wise and good; she will advise us.'

'Aye, I'll tell Pery mysel'. I'll awa to Eildon Ha'.' Croudy went off with Mumps following. Gale let him go and himself went back with his sheep to the fold, then to the Hall.

Pery was one of the maids at the Hall, a fine, cheerful lass who had half the lads in the place sighing after her. To one only had she given her heart – to Gale, who was friendly and gallant, but so far nothing more. Gale liked the lassies, and he could have had his pick, for he had gallant words and smiles for all of them, but he never went too far – not as far indeed as some would have liked. Pery tried to lure him on by teasing. Croudy had small interest in any of them; he was a dour, rather stupid fellow. Pery did not care a scrap for him, but out of sheer mischief she made up to him and led him on in order, she hoped, to rouse Gale to at least a flicker of jealousy.

Croudy may not have cared much for her or any other girl, but he had his full share of vanity and was very ready to believe that Pery was in love with him. When he came to Eildon Hall, he went to find her.

'I ha'e a tale to tell that will surprise ye,' he said. 'Meet me at the Moss Thorn when the milkin's done.'

'I'll do that,' Pery promised cheerfully. 'But it's no' likely you'll surprise me. I'll wager you three kisses that I can guess what you have to tell.'

Croudy grunted and went off, while Pery went to the milking with the other maids.

At the Abbey Walk two ladies were talking together, two sisters very like each other, of great loveliness but with a strange, ethereal kind of beauty, a certain wildness in their looks, as if they were not wholly of this world but partly of fairy. They were dressed in white.

'We have been seen and heard, dear Ellen,' said one. 'That clown who lay hidden in the branches of the Eildon tree and watched us will gossip and do mischief. Our work is not yet done. We must prevent him.'

'Indeed, dear Clara, we must. We have still our greatest task to do, this very night. The plot is laid against the King. Lord Angus is in it, and the Abbot himself. We have no love for the King, but we must guard him.'

'Indeed we must, so you stay close by him, Ellen. I shall come back as soon as I have dealt with that fellow. Give me our magic wand. I know where to find him.'

The Lady Clara took the wand and walked swiftly away to the Moss Thorn. Croudy lay there on the grass, Mumps beside him, awaiting Pery. He saw a lady in a white gown come towards him.

'Fegs, Pery's deckit hersel' in her best to meet me,' he thought complacently. 'She's bonny, I'll say that. And she loo's me.' He chuckled.

The lady came and stood over him. She struck him three times with her wand and uttered strange words, and there in place of rough Croudy lay a great ugly boar. The lady departed as swiftly as she had come. Croudy lay growling in rage and fear, for he was still himself, inside the boar, aware that he had been bewitched but believing that it was Pery who had touched him.

'Fause witch that she is,' he growled and groaned. 'If ever I get free, I'll ha'e her burned for sorcery.'

Poor Mumps lay shivering with fear. Then, as Croudy the boar began groaning in misery, the faithful beast crept close to him, whining pitifully and licking his face as he lay down beside him, for some dim instinct told him that the boar was his master. They lay like this for quite a while, then slowly and laboriously the boar rose to his feet and lumbered off, followed closely by Mumps. He made for Eildon Hall. He must find Pery and somehow compel her to change him back into his true form. Nothing would convince him that it was not she who had bewitched him.

In the meadow behind the Hall the maids were busy milking, but when the boar appeared, all the cows ran away; there was a wild scattering, the maids cried out, some of the men in the place came running. The boar fled to a field where the corn grew thick and sank down in a furrow. The men were ready to attack, but things began to quieten, the cows returned, the maids went back to their milking. Croudy rose from his hiding-place and went back to the Moss Thorn, still followed by Mumps. Croudy was famished with hunger, but there was nothing to eat, and presently they both fell asleep. In the morning he went back to the courtyard of the Hall. No one bothered about him, for now he seemed quiet and harmless enough; it was felt that he must belong to someone and have wandered away; they would have him proclaimed at the market cross, and his owner would claim him.

No one could quite understand how Mumps came to be with the boar, but no one was very concerned, except Pery, who said kindly: 'Mumps, poor fellow, come you in and I'll give you something to eat.' But Mumps would not leave the boar, so Pery brought out a great bowl of cold porridge.

Mumps would not touch it until the boar had eaten his fill, then he cleared the dish. 'Good Mumps,' said Pery cheerfully.

Up at the abbey much had happened, and not all of it good. One of the King's white hounds, Mooly, had followed her master into the refectory and would not be turned out.

'Let her stay,' said the King. 'You see she will not leave me. She will lie quietly beside me.'

The table was set with rich food and excellent claret. 'And for you, my lord,' said the Abbot genially, 'there is a bottle of your favourite malmsey.' He spoke to one of the servants: 'Ralph, here is the key of the cellar. Bring the bottle of malmsey and fill the King's cup.'

Ralph obeyed, and the King rose, holding the full cup: 'Fill your own cups, my lords, and drink to the toast I propose.' They filled their cups with claret and stood respectfully. 'To the fairest lady in my kingdom,' proclaimed the King. 'The Lady Ellen of Roslin.'

The company stood amazed for a moment; then each man raised his cup to drink. The King lifted his own, full of malmsey. Before he could touch it with his lips, however, Mooly sprang and knocked it from his hand, splashing the wine all over the floor. What a fuss there was! 'Turn that hound out! Away with her, see that she is given a good thrashing.'

'Let her stay,' commanded the King.

'Bring another cup for His Grace,' the Abbot told Ralph. Again the King stood, again lifted the cup to his lips, again Mooly sprang and knocked it out of his hand.

'Let me have some claret,' commanded the King. The Abbot looked pale and shaken, as did some others of the company.

Ralph brought a cup of claret; the King raised it to his lips. Mooly lay still at his feet. He drank and sat down.

'But Your Grace must have some of your favourite,' the Abbot told him. 'There is another bottle of the malmsey. Fetch it, Ralph.'

Ralph obeyed and filled the King's cup.

'Drink this yourself,' the King told him.

Obediently Ralph lifted the cup, and drank. Presently he withdrew to a window seat, looking pale and ill.

'What ails you, Ralph?' asked one of the company who sat near him.

'I do not know. I feel ill. The wine does not agree with my stomach.'

Poor Ralph spoke very feebly, and even as he spoke he swayed and fell forward, his face transfused with blood. The man who had spoken to him went to lift him.

'God be with him. God help us, he is dead.'

'Poison,' shouted another. 'Look to the doors,' cried a third. 'There is treason here.'

Lord Douglas bolted and barred the door and stood before it with drawn sword. There was a storm of shouting, of accusation and counter-accusation.

'I am innocent,' cried Angus.

'It was that villain Ralph who did this foul deed,' declared the Abbot in a trembling voice. His face was pallid. 'He alone had charge of the bottles.'

'That I do not believe,' declared the King. 'He drank without fear or hesitation. God rest him. He is the victim of a foul plot laid against myself.'

There was more uproar.

'What of yourself, my lord Abbot?' cried more than one. 'It was from your cellar that the malmsey came, and by your order.'

The Abbot protested his innocence: 'An enemy, God knows who, God forgive him, must have broken into the cellar.'

For the moment his word was accepted, and the tumult died down. The dead body was carried out. The King spoke not a word, and in silence he withdrew to his own room. There he spoke to a trusted servant whom he sent to summon a troop of Border troopers to be his guard and escort next day, when he would ride back to Edinburgh. He was followed by Mooly and by her sister hound Scratch, who had suddenly appeared from outside. The King locked his door, and trusted servants stood outside, on guard while he said his rosary.

Next morning he heard Mass. As he was leaving the chapel, he was told that a suppliant waited in the courtyard, to speak to him. The suppliant was the old man who had appeared so suddenly on the Eildon hill, at the hunt, and as suddenly disappeared. With him were two women, weeping bitterly.

'Justice, my lord King,' he cried. 'Justice and vengeance for these poor mothers whose children have been carried away in the night, killed and devoured by those evil hounds.'

'That cannot be,' the King replied sternly. 'They were with me, in my room, all night; the door was locked and guarded, the window barred. Let my guards be summoned.'

The two men who had stood outside the King's room came. The King asked them if they had kept watch all night, the door fast locked. The men looked at each other uneasily. They had indeed kept awake and watchful, and they had heard no sound. The door had been fast shut, but in the early morning the two hounds had suddenly appeared, from whence the men could not tell, nor how they had got out.

'There is strange evil at work here,' declared the King.

As he spoke, another woman came into the courtyard: an aged dame, very stately, in a rich dress long out of fashion, with hooped skirts and ruff and head-dress. The old man greeted her with deference. She wept and spoke to the King in rage and grief.

'My lord King, I demand justice and aid. My daughter, my only daughter, has been taken from me by sorcery. These evil hounds have taken her.'

The King looked, but there was no sign of Mooly or of Scratch. Then an old monk, a good and holy man, who was convinced of the presence of evil, came forward carrying a vessel of holy water. The King was questioning the old dame, and the old man was defending her, declaring her to be a most worthy gentlewoman. But some of the monks were muttering that both she and her daughter were of ill repute, suspected of witchcraft. Suddenly the sacristan threw some drops of holy water on the old dame and on the old man. The woman shrieked horribly; the old man gave a wild and fiendish yell and, in his true form of the foul fiend himself, rose into the air and flew away.

The old woman, her face hideously contorted, lay writhing like a serpent on the ground. The two young women fell on their knees, weeping, imploring pardon, imploring leave to make their confession. The sacristan sprinkled some drops of holy water upon them too, so that they trembled, then grew calm. The sacristan made the sign of the cross over them and they knelt there, weeping in contrition.

They told how they had been tempted by the old dame and her daughter, both well advanced in sorcery. The fiend himself had come, in the form of a young and handsome man, and had forced them to agree, under threat of being denounced as witches, to tell this story of the theft of their children, who had indeed been taken away.

'Have you and your children been baptized?' asked the sacristan. They had not.

'Will you accept holy baptism now, for yourselves and for your children when they are found?'

'We will indeed.'

So they were led into the chapel, where they made their confessions, received absolution and were baptized.

The old dame was seized, bound and taken before the court, uttering dreadful curses. She was condemned and before the day was over was burned at the stake. As the flames were lit, the fiend their master appeared again, yelling in mockery, then flying away.

It should be added that the children had indeed been taken away – by the hounds, or by the ladies, taken to a place of safety, where they were found sound asleep. They were brought back to their mothers, baptized and blessed, and the two young women went home in tears of humility and thankfulness.

The King with all his company left the abbey and rode to Edinburgh. The white hounds ran by his horse for some miles beyond the Eildons, then they disappeared. None could say exactly when or where, but they were never seen again.

In a green lane near the abbey, the two sisters stood and talked. There was something strange about their appearance, but they were indeed beautiful and they seemed to be at peace in the world.

'The King is safe, the witches of Eildon are destroyed, and our work is done. Thanks to our care in hiding the children safely, they are now home with their mothers. Now we may go home to our own beloved mother, alone and sad in her widowhood.'

'Have we left all in order? What of that clown you enchanted? Is he still held in the form of a boar?'

'He is, and he may remain thus until he is killed and devoured.'

'Will you not have pity on him, sister? He can do no harm now, however much he may gossip about what he saw.'

'As you will; you are kinder than I.'

The Lady Clara took the wand and walked swiftly off to Eildon Hall. There was indeed something to be done there. No one had claimed the boar, so the master of Eildon Hall had decided to put him up for sale. There he lay in the yard, fast bound with ropes. The maids, remembering the fright he had given them, had each lent a garter to help to tie him, Pery among them. She was far from being unkind, but like the others she saw only a rough boar that might have done harm.

A purchaser was not long in coming. The stores in the abbey had been greatly depleted by the royal visit, and Gudgel the cook was worried. News of the boar came as a great relief to him, so he hurried into the yard behind the hall and looked at the captive with approval.

'There is fine meat indeed for many a meal and for store. The Abbot will gladly pay.'

The price was agreed, and Gudgel went off to fetch the butcher, while everyone else left the yard to go about their own work. Only faithful Mumps stayed with the wretched Croudy. Then came the lady in white whom he had seen before. Swiftly she came and touched him with her wand three times, speaking strange words. Then she departed as swiftly as she had come, and Croudy saw himself in his own true shape, while Mumps whimpered in delight and licked his face and hands.

At that moment Gudgel came back with the butcher. They stood amazed but not incredulous, for witchcraft was only too well known there, and too much had happened, too many strange tales had been told in the past two or three days, to make this appear a miracle out of the common. The butcher cut the bonds with his sharp knife. Croudy stood up, in great relief and great anger.

'She'll pay for this, that witch,' he growled.

'Wha was it that did this to you, Croudy?' asked the butcher.

'It was that lass Pery. She may luik bonny, she may speak ye fair, but she's as wicked a witch as ony o' them that were taken. Lat her be taken noo and brought to justice.'

The news spread. The household came running, neighbours gathered, the men came from the fields, as Croudy told his tale of the witch's coming to enchant him and later to change him back again. That witch he swore and believed to be Pery. At first few believed this. Pery was well liked for her kindness and cheerfulness. But other proven witches had shown charm. There were two main types of women led into sorcery: the old hags of bitter temper, and the young, beautiful and lively ones who were ripe for mischief. Some of the witches recently burnt had been like that. Slowly belief in Croudy's tale spread, and people drew away from poor Pery. She was taken and tried, condemned to death and thrust into prison.

No one pitied her but Gale. He heard the tale, but not a word of it did he believe. No matter how convinced Croudy might be of Pery's guilt, Gale knew that it was impossible. He was quite certain of her innocence, and indeed of her genuine kindliness. Unlike his neighbours he was not prone to superstition, and he was gentle and just. He had always been fond of Pery, though not so deeply in love with her as she with him. But now fondness and compassion together grew to profound love. He must save Pery.

Gale went to the prison and begged to be admitted. The gaoler let him in, for he himself pitied the poor lass and was more than half convinced of her innocence. As he entered, Gale crossed himself and spoke the Holy Name. Pery, who lay weeping, looked up and in her turn made the sign of the cross.

'Will you say the Our Father with me?' Gale asked gently.

'I will, and gladly.'

Together they said the prayer, kneeling side by side in the prison.

'I shall not leave you, Pery, my love. I know you are innocent. Perhaps I cannot save you, but I can at least stay with you.'

'That is comfort enough, dear Gale; that and the knowledge that you hold me innocent.'

No one disturbed them, and they talked together for a while, and when dusk fell, they lay asleep in each other's arms.

Once again the ladies Clara and Ellen were walking together.

'Well, that clown is free,' said Clara. 'But he is cruel and vengeful . . . he has brought that innocent girl to grief, and it seems that nothing now can save her from a cruel death.'

'We can save her,' said Ellen. 'Let us go now to the prison.'

So they walked to the prison, where they spoke courteously to the gaoler, begging leave to enter. He gave it gladly and opened the door. For a moment they stood looking with compassion at the sleeping lovers.

'Here is innocence, here is faith, here is true love,' they murmured.

Clara touched the lovers with her wand. From the floor of the cell rose two beautiful moorfowl, cock and hen.

'We cannot save them otherwise,' said Clara, 'but as birds they will be free.'

The birds fluttered up to the roof, fluttered down again, let themselves be taken and held each by one of the ladies, sheltered under their cloaks. The ladies left the cell, bowed graciously to the gaoler, gave him a gold piece and walked out, beyond the walls, out beyond the fields and up the hill. There they released the moorfowl, who flew up and away together, away into freedom.

Then at last the ladies returned to Roslin, to find their dear, sad, widowed mother. But she was no longer sad, no longer widowed. She had taken a new husband, a baron, some called him a pirate, a man of great strength and wealth if little kindness, but they were obviously fond of each other. There was clearly no place for her daughters there, so they departed no one knows where. There was fairy blood in them, and it is likely that they went to the land of those other kinsfolk, beyond this earth, for no mortal eyes saw them again in this world.

Source:
James Hogg, *The Ettrick Shepherd's Tales*

The Witches of Traquair

'Traquair was a terrible place then. There was a witch in almost every hamlet, and a warlock here and there besides.' So James Hogg the Ettrick Shepherd begins his tale, and what he did not know about witches and warlocks, forbye brownies and other queer folk, would be worth finding out; but there is enough here to be going on with.

It happened on the eve of the Reformation. The old religion was still in power, Cardinal Beaton ruled the Church from St Andrews, the valiant Mary of Guise was Regent, and young Queen Mary was still in France.

The power of the Church was waning, much to the delight of the Devil and his agents, for that one has a keen eye for human lapses, for doubts and insecurity in the human mind, for the lust for power. He is quick to find agents, and the agents in their turn must be eydent about finding helpers.

Young Colin Hyslop the shepherd was a good enough lad, though weak. He would have been better and stronger had his good father lived, for he had been a man of strong faith and deep wisdom. He had warned Colin against the temptations and evils he saw threatening him, for he had foreseen evil times, and he knew who the evil folk were. But his good father was dead, and Colin had no mother – she had died when he was a baby – and no kin on his father's side. His closest relation was his Auntie Nance, and she was a known witch, in fact head of the local coven, and her chief confederate was a certain Robert Kirkwood, a warlock. With all the power of their evil wills, they wanted to draw others into their circle, within the power of Satan; most of all they wanted Colin.

They had almost won. Colin was weak in will; he had no strong faith. As a child he had occasionally gone to Mass, but it had little effect on him; nor had the teaching and prayers of his father. The influence was there but overlaid and over-shadowed by the mirk of wizardry. Auntie Nance was truly, as some folk said, 'the wickedest witch in Christendye'.

She and the warlock had given Colin a scroll to sign with his blood. There was a sign of the cross on the scroll; this he must blot out with his blood, then make the sign of the crescent in its place. Already he was on the way, for he was much in their powers. Already they had bewitched him – changing into the form of a goat and of a ram. He had seen strange and terrible things, wild dances, and his poor sheep had been bewitched. Some of them were dead, though not before he had seen them dancing hornpipes and cotillions, like creatures under enchantment and wild compulsion.

Colin was in deep distress and perplexity. He had begun to see witchcraft everywhere, to suspect every woman of being a witch, even his sweetheart, Barbara. *Was* Barbara a witch? Would she lead him astray?

He sat on the hillside, with the sheep that were left to him and with his good dog, Bawty. He had drawn blood from his arm and dipped a quill in it, ready to obliterate the cross and make the sign of the crescent.

Suddenly there appeared two beautiful white hinds. All the huntsman in Colin was stirred. The land here was out of the royal boundary, so he might safely pursue and kill. There was Bawty – but Bawty would not stir, and the deer left no scent. Bawty lay quivering beside him, though without showing any evidence of terror. Could the white hinds be witches?

He took up the scroll. There was no trace of his blood on it, no crescent, but the cross was plainly marked. Surely the two white hinds could not be witches? Perhaps they were angels come to save him.

Strange things were happening. The white deer passed again. Could they have come to save him? There was the scroll, unstained, bearing the clear mark of the cross. There was time yet, time to remember his good father's warning. But there was danger too, for the witches would take a fearful vengeance if he opposed them.

Colin saw two hares running. Without thought, he ran after them, shouting to Bawty to follow, but that wise dog would not come. He cowered in fear. Colin went on alone, in great fear. He knew that the hares were evil, probably Nance and Robert Kirkwood in disguise. Colin was terrified but found himself unable to pray.

Two ladies in white gowns came towards Colin. They were lovely and kind-looking and moved swiftly and lightly over the field. Bawty lay very quiet, with no shudder or whimper of fear, but as if in awe. The ladies looked at Colin, who stopped and bowed awkwardly. Their looks and their words were at once compassionate and stern. They warned him of his deadly peril, of a danger far beyond any violence to his body. Colin wept, vowing his contrition, imploring their help.

One of the ladies gave him a small bottle. 'Drink, and you will be changed,' she said – but for Colin this could only mean such change as he had known before, into the shape of a goat or a ram or a hare. He wanted to refuse the bottle.

'It will do you no harm. It is no poison. The change will not be in your body,' one lady told him, and the other: 'We have come to help you, to set you free, but you must obey.'

Colin drank a little from the bottle, finding the taste very bitter, yet he felt it cleansing.

'You must drink again and yet again,' they said. Sternly they looked into his eyes, yet with an expression of infinite compassion, before moving swiftly and lightly away.

Colin was left alone with Bawty, who came creeping up to him and licked his hand and looked at him with faithful, trusting eyes. He found tears coursing down his cheeks as he took another drink from the little bottle – which oddly enough still seemed to be full to the brim. The taste was extremely bitter, but he no longer feared that it might be poison. He rose from the ground and walked home with Bawty close upon his heels.

The two hares had taken their own human form, as Nance

and Kirkwood, and they lay hidden behind a great bush talking their evil thoughts.

'Kimmer, he's oors, he's oors,' the warlock said exultingly. 'We've won the prize. The maister will be gey pleased. He hes aye wantit Colin. Och, luik at the blude he's shed, the bonny, bonny blude!'

'Aye, he's oors,' said the witch Nance. 'Since the day he was born, I've wanted this, I've worked for this.'

'An noo we'll up and owre the kirk tower wi' him. Och, the bonny rid blude!'

'What think ye o' thae twa deer, Rob? I mislike them. They're no' canny.'

'Och, what need ye mind of them, kimmer? They can dae nocht. Luik at the blude, the bonny blude. I like weel to see Christian blude, kimmer. It bodes luck to us.'

'Rob, Rob, I'm no' sae sure o' that. I dinna like their luik. Rob, Rob, do ye see – he's boo'ed doun to the grun, he's in tears. We've lost him, Rob, thae deer ha'e dune something. Och, Rob, luik, they are nae deer – they are twa leddies – wha they are I daurna say, I daurna think. But we've lost him, and the Maister will tak' his vengeance on us.'

Their maister came – in what shape none ever knew, and it were best not to seek to find out. Next morning their cronies came to find them, and found them battered and torn as if by the fiercest of wild animals. They were very near death, and both of them died while being carried home. Their burial was in no consecrated ground.

Colin went home with his faithful Bawty, and again he drank from the wee bottle, which was still full to the brim of its bitter but heart-warming fluid. Again he saw the two beautiful ladies, who smiled at him with a heavenly radiance.

Colin went to talk to his sweetheart, Barbara. Now he was quite sure that there was no taint or shadow of witchcraft about her, so he went to her humbly, and she received him with gentle love. He knew that she was as good as she was bonny, and as brave as she was good. She would defend him in need, with the valour of her own patron, St Barbara.

Soon after this he again met the two ladies, who gave him to wear round his neck a medal of gold which seemed to glow red, as if it had been dipped in blood. This would guard him against all harm, and indeed he had need of it.

On the day of the burial of Nance and Rob Kirkwood, Colin was attacked by a horde of wild cats, at the junction of the Quair water with a little burn called the Satyr Sike. Colin was mauled by the cats, but he fought back, and brave Bawty came to his help, though he was badly hurt. Yet any cat that touched the medal he wore under his shirt fell back howling in agony. Colin defended himself well, and when one creature attacked again and again, he struck her with his crook and broke her paw. Next morning Maude Stott, the new leader of the coven, lay helpless with a broken leg. Finally the two ladies appeared and the horde of cats fled. Again they looked kindly upon Colin, again he bowed low, thanked them and promised to drink from the bottle and cherish the medal.

That night the foul fiend himself tried to enter Colin's cottage while he lay sleepless and quivering in terror. He was unable either to think or to pray. Then the memory of his good father came back, filling his mind; and with the thought of that father came, very slowly and with difficulty, the words of the Our Father.

Colin did not know that he was protected, for one of the ladies stood outside the door, keeping watch and ward; but Barbara knew. She had come out to look and listen, fearing that Colin was in deadly danger. There at the door she saw that lovely, queenly figure in white, and she curtseyed low. The lady looked at her with great loving kindness, and Barbara went home, in peace and thankfulness.

The fiend and his minions had one weapon left. The witches and warlocks denounced Colin for witchcraft, with a fine convincing tale, and he was brought to trial. With the presiding judge sat Cardinal Beaton himself, most formidable of all opponents. He felt certain of Colin's guilt and resolved to bring him to the final punishment.

One witness declared that he had seen Colin turn into a goat, then back again to his true form. Another had pursued a fox, with his hounds; when he came up with the hounds, there was Colin amongst them, pacifying them. The goat had come into the kirk and ramped about. The priest had prayed against him in Latin, but still he had rampaged around. Some of the men had attacked him with their sticks, battering and wounding him, and next day Colin was found bruised. Then suddenly the tide began slowly to turn. The hostility against Colin changed to suspicion of the witnesses. Several of them were suspected or known witches and warlocks. Colin was liked for his own sake, as his father had been. He was a douce, quiet lad who had done nothing to injure or offend anyone. He was honest, too, and did not deny that he might have been seen in the form of a fox or a goat or other beast, for he had been under the power of the witches. That was known, and there was pity for him rather than reprobation.

Then someone muttered: 'Let the saddle be laid on the richt horse' – meaning, let guilt be placed on the real offenders. Hostility receded from Colin and mounted against the witnesses. There was a cry that the whole company of them, witches and warlocks, be held and tried. They were all in the court, so let them be taken before they could escape. The Cardinal was still against Colin, but the laird, Sir James Stuart of Traquair, defended him, maintaining that he had been sorely troubled by the power of the witches, by their avenging fury because he would not yield and join their company.

The old sacristan of the kirk called out: 'Tak' and haud the limmers, or they will turn themselves into moorfowl and paitricks, blatterin' about the riggin' o' the kirk.'

The Cardinal and the presiding magistrate yielded so far as to order the arrest of the suspect witches and warlocks. They were summarily tried and condemned to be burned to death. Then they ordered Colin to be searched, which soon revealed the medal and the little bottle. The medal could not be removed, but the bottle was handed to the judge, who declared that it contained a magic potion, ample proof of Colin's guilt.

'Not so,' said a wise and godly old man in the court. 'This is a bottle of repentance.' He then looked carefully at the medal hung round Colin's neck. On one side were engraved the words: 'Forgiveness; Acceptance.' On the other was an effigy of Our Lord on the cross, with the words: '*Cruci, dum vivo, fido.*'

There had been much questioning about the two beautiful

ladies who had come to Colin. Were they fairies, or rather guardian spirits, holy and benign? The Cardinal was by now almost convinced of Colin's innocence and asked: 'Did either of these ladies resemble the picture of Our Lady that hangs there?'

Everyone looked at the holy picture, and brave Barbara rose and cried out: 'The Lady I saw at Colin's door, guarding it, was wondrous like.'

The Cardinal capitulated, and Colin was set free at once. The Cardinal took him back to Edinburgh and presented him to the Queen Regent, who, greatly moved by his story, gave him money and land and sheep, and a dowry for Barbara. Other gifts were made him by a monastery, so that he was well set up for life. Barbara and he were married and lived to their lives' end in love and happiness, they and their children. All that Colin did prospered well.

We are not told any more about the two fair ladies. Hogg wondered whether they were the personification of Faith and Charity. One was lame, and no one could think of any explanation of that. Could it be that one of the ladies was really the Mother of God, the other an attendant – possibly Colin's own guardian angel or patron saint, or perhaps St Barbara, who would have a tenderness for that good lass her namesake and for her sweetheart? For myself, I choose to believe that the guardian of Colin's door and cottage was Our Lady herself.

Source:
James Hogg, *The Ettrick Shepherd's Tales*

Dragons

The Laidly Worm of
Spindleston Heugh

This tale was told by a wandering minstrel in the castle of a Northumbrian chief. It is a good story of adventure, danger and courage, of challenge, witchcraft (of a kind), a lovely princess, a wicked stepmother, a brave lover – and a happy, surprising and even comic ending. It tells of a time when the old gods of the north were not forgotten. Odin is still worshipped, and he is a constant presence in the background. Through his protection the King, Ethelfrith, is victorious in battle.

King Ethelfrith was honoured for his courage but more feared for his ferocity than loved for any virtue. The hearts of his people were wholly given to his Queen, who was lovely and gentle, and to their daughter Agitha, who had all her mother's beauty and kindness. But the beloved Queen died.

The Princess Agitha had many wooers, men of valour, of high rank and rich possessions. To one only did she give her heart, and that was her cousin the Chylde Wynde. (*Chylde*, a word used in many old tales and ballads, means a youth of noble birth; as we would say 'Lord' or 'Prince'.)

The King approved the betrothal between his daughter and his nearest kinsman, the heir presumptive, but he made one condition. Whoever married the Princess must bring another realm to add to the kingdom which already stretched from Tyne to Forth, to the fort of Dunedin.

'Bring me a crown in your left hand,' he told the Chylde, 'and I will place my daughter's hand in your right, in betrothal.'

The Chylde accepted the challenge. 'But will you swear to me that you will let no other wooer, even if he have a crown to offer, be with the Princess in my absence?'

This enraged the King. He stamped his iron-shod foot until all the armour and weapons which hung in the hall clanged and rang.

'Do you dare try to bargain with me – the descendant of Woden, your king? Go, before I spill your blood upon the floor.'

The Chylde controlled his own wrath, left the King and went to take leave of the Princess, his beloved. She wept at the thought of his departure, but she was as brave as she was gentle and would not hold him back. They vowed eternal faith to each other. The Chylde summoned his host of warriors, and they sailed away in their galleys. Agitha looked after them from the cliff, until the last speck of sail had vanished.

She was very brave, and the people loved her more than ever. Chylde Wynde was a hero to them, and they looked forward confidently to his return. The Princess was lovelier than ever; there was no other lady to match her, and none of them grudged her the homage paid to her, none was jealous – except one, who came near her in beauty: Bethoc, the daughter of the thane Gormac who was a noted wizard as well as a rich and powerful noble. In Bethoc's beauty there was enchantment, but not of a good kind. The King heard of her, saw her and was captivated. He would make her his Queen. Bethoc was very willing to accept, for she had indeed schemed for it, putting a spell upon the King, helped by her father. She had been jealous of the dead Queen and had vowed to be her successor, and jealous of the Princess and vowed to displace both her and the Chylde Wynde. She would bear the King a son, many sons, and that nephew would have no place in the succession, even if he brought back half a dozen crowns.

So Ethelfrith and Bethoc were married and came home to

the royal castle with its great tower. Agitha went to meet her
stepmother with courtesy and kindness. The people were less
courteous; they dared not show hostility, but they could be
lukewarm in their welcome. The minstrels were less than
lukewarm. They sang, with formal flattery, of the new
Queen's beauty, hailing her as a brilliant star of evening, one of
a splendid constellation. Then they sang of their own Princess
as a star of morning, shining alone in the heavens, beautiful,
radiant beyond compare.

This pleased the people, who whispered and murmured the
words, laughing and nodding their heads. It did not please the
Queen at all, and her rage and jealousy robbed her of every
trace of beauty. She spoke bitterly to the Princess, who knelt in
homage: 'Rise, Princess. You must not kneel to me who am but
one of a host of stars, you who are the star of morning,
supreme in beauty.'

The coldness and venom of her voice and look froze those
who heard and saw her. The King, more notable for courage
and ferocity than for any great powers of perception, noticed
nothing.

Now there lived in that neighbourhood in a cave above the
sea a woman reputed to be a powerful witch, one Elgiva. The
cave was a dreadful place of darkness, inhabited by fearsome
creatures, bats and toads. Two owls sat within, each upon a
skull, their eyes giving the only light. There were many stories
of the witch's power, yet oddly enough there was not a trace of
evidence of any evil that she might have done.

Among those who held her to be very powerful was the
thane Gormac, father of the Queen, so when the Queen went
to her father to demand that he put a cruel spell upon the
Princess, changing her shape and holding her bound, he
refused.

'I dare not. The King would suspect and would take dire
vengeance. But go now to the witch Elgiva who dwells in her
cave. Surely you can persuade her to work her magic against
the Princess. Go – but tell me nothing about it. I must be able to
say that I know nothing.'

Bethoc went to the cave and summoned the witch-woman.
Elgiva stood at the door, darkness behind her, strange shapes

flitting and crawling. While the Queen spoke harshly and without courtesy, the witch-woman listened, with head bowed.

'You will change the Princess into whatever shape you will,' the Queen ordered, 'and you will hold her here as your prisoner, unless you can train her to roam about doing harm. And you will say nothing of this to anyone. If you refuse, I shall have you taken and tortured.'

The woman raised her head, gave the Queen a very strange look, bowed and spoke: 'Bring the Princess here to me, then depart.'

The Queen went home, summoned the Princess and ordered her to come with her to the cave. She had two servants, a rough pair who had come with her from her father's house, walk behind. The poor Princess protested, pleaded and tried to escape, but the servants held her.

At the entrance to the cave the witch-woman awaited them. 'Enter,' she bade the Princess. 'And you depart,' she told the Queen and her attendants. 'Come again in seven days' time and you will see what you will see.' The Queen departed. In the cave the Princess fainted. The witch-woman revived her, spoke to her, uttered strange words and continued a work she had begun.

The Queen gave out that the Princess was ill, pining for her lover. In seven days, she went back to the cave. On the threshold lay a laidly worm, a great loathsome serpent with scaly skin, coiled up. The witch-woman stood behind.

'You see what I have done,' she told the Queen. 'So now depart, and come here no more.'

The evil Queen went home and began to spread a new rumour about the Princess: that she had fled and was following her lover, the Chylde Wynde, and that neither of them would ever return. The King accepted this, for he was still bewitched and besotted by his evil wife. He had never had any deep affection for his daughter and had always been jealous of his nephew. Let them go, let them stay where they would, beyond his realm. His new Queen would bear him a son, many sons, to follow him.

The people did not believe the rumour. Even if they had,

they would not have blamed the Princess for escaping, for seeking her lover, who was greatly liked and honoured, whom the people would gladly have as their King. Then other strange events happened.

There was this laidly worm, lying at the entrance to the witch's cave: a fearsome creature, to be shunned. Yet there was no news of its attacking people or seizing and devouring cattle or sheep. It was just seen to lie there, right at the front of the witch-woman's cave. A new rumour began to be whispered. Might the witch have enchanted the Princess into this dreadful shape? Yet even in that form the Princess could never be cruel. No spell could touch her gentle spirit. The mystery deepened; there were mutterings and whisperings, yet none dared carry any rumour to the King.

Meanwhile Chylde Wynde and his host had come to a realm where the King was a tyrant, detested by his subjects. There had been a battle, brief and victorious for the Chylde, the tyrant slain, the people thankful to be free. Then the Chylde took the crown and with his host sailed for home. At once he walked up to the castle, into the hall, into the presence of Ethelfrith, carrying the new crown in his left hand.

'Here is your crown,' he said. 'Now keep your word and bring the Princess Agitha to lay her hand in mind, in betrothal.'

The King looked bewildered, overwhelmed, dismayed. 'She is not here. She has fled,' he muttered. Chylde Wynde looked at him with contempt, turned and walked from the hall. There were many people outside, there were whispers, the voices grew louder; there was a great welcome for the Chylde, their Prince and possibly soon to be their King. He demanded to know all that had happened, and one old man, one of the minstrels, told him:

'We know not, for certain, my lord, but we believe that the Lady Agitha, our beloved Princess, has been enchanted. Bethoc is known to have gone to the witch who dwells in the cave yonder. She spread rumours that the Princess was ill, then that she had fled. Then a strange creature appeared at the cave, a laidly worm, and some believe that this is our Princess enchanted by the witch, under compulsion by Bethoc.'

The Chylde marched straight to the cave, sword in hand. At

the entrance lay the loathsome creature, coiled, glittering, and behind it stood the witch-woman.

'Witch, sorceress, I command you to undo the evil you have done. Release from enchantment, from your evil power, the Princess my beloved, or your life will not be long.'

The woman looked at him calmly. 'Put up your sword. The Princess is safe. Be calm, my son; you cannot attack the mother who bore you.'

The Chylde stared, gasped and dropped his sword. 'My mother! But what do you mean?'

'You remember your father, but you do not know the whole story, for who dared to tell you it? Your father died in battle, but there was treachery in his slaying. The King Ethelfrith hated his brother, who was loved by the people, and he wanted me. I was comely enough then. He would not harm you; he had no son, so he was quite happy to accept you as his heir; you were quite safe. But for me there was only this escape, into the shadows of the cave, into the darkness of rumour, of reputed witchcraft. I have done harm to none, but rumour and fear have protected me. And when that evil woman came to me, commanding that I transform the Princess, I obeyed. But she is here, your love. These are but fish-skins I have sewn together as disguise.'

The witch-woman was smiling now, her look very kind. She stooped over the serpent and spoke very gently and lovingly. 'Loosen your disguise and come forth, my dear, my daughter.'

There was a rustling, and the head of the serpent began to move. Elgiva knelt and put her hands to the head; slowly the head of the Princess emerged. The Chylde shouted with joy, knelt down, took his sword and very gently, very deftly, began cutting the folds of fish-skin. Soon they all fell away, and he lifted Agitha gently to her feet and held her in his arms. Then he embraced his mother, who no longer looked forbidding. She was indeed comely, kind and gentle.

Many people had followed him, so the news spread and there was a tumult of joy and laughter. They all turned back towards the castle.

When the Chylde had left there, the evil Queen had climbed to the top of the tower to watch. Now she saw the returning procession, heard the shouts of joy, the beginning of songs by the minstrels, the laughter. Her end would be death. She took her own way, hurling herself from that high tower, and none mourned her.

The King was overwhelmed. He could only accept and acknowledge his son-in-law his heir, realizing the Queen's guilt. The marriage was celebrated at once, with a great feast.

Soon after that King Ethelfrith went again into battle. Always before he had fought under the protection of his ancestor, Woden the god. But Woden was just and he hated treachery. He withdrew his protection; he would not look upon the King, and in that battle Ethelfrith was slain.

There were few who mourned him, but all the people welcomed the new King and his bride, the beloved Agitha, and hardly less warmly did they welcome and honour the Queen Mother, Elgiva, once reputed a witch. There were many tales for the minstrels to tell and sing and pass down. This was a long and happy reign, and there were sons and daughters of the marriage who inherited the love and honour paid to their parents.

Source:
J. M. Wilson and Alexander Leighton, *Tales of the Borders*

The Worm of Linton

Great worms or dragons recur in Border legend. The Laidly Worm of Spindleston Heugh was, in the end, not so loathsome after all. But at Linton in Roxburghshire there was a fearsome specimen: the Worm of Linton.

Linton is a bonny part of the country, with green fields and hills, woods beyond, and in the distance the great Cheviots. It should have been peaceful, but there was little peace when the great and loathsome worm or dragon harassed the land. He lay in his den in a dark hollow. He did not often come out, as some dragons did to sweep and devour; he had little need to move. Lying in his den, he breathed out fire and poisonous smoke that touched the sheep and cattle, then drew in his breath and, with it, the poor half-dead creatures which he devoured. The shepherds were lucky if they escaped without being drawn in themselves. They were none of them unscathed: they were scorched often, in skin and hair. They were left coughing, throat and lungs tainted.

When he did come out of his dark den, he would curl himself in great scaly coils round a low green knowe, and none dare come near. There were prayers for deliverance, prayers for a champion who could slay the monster. But who could come near him, and what use was the sharpest sword or spear? They would hardly scratch that tough hide. Courage was not lacking – and at last came a valiant man, the Laird o' Linton, whose courage was equalled by his sense and resource.

He wore no armour, carried no shield, for none would have protected him against that breath of fire and venom. The dragon lay coiled round the knowe. The Laird rode carrying a long lance on which he had thrust a peat soaked in burning pitch. The dragon reared his loathsome head and opened his huge jaws to breathe forth fire and venom, but the brave and canny Laird got in first. He thrust the fiery peat into the gaping mouth, down into the burning throat. The monster choked horribly. The fiery, venomous breath came slowly, feebly. The Laird sat firm on his horse, thrust the lance still deeper, held it firm.

All around and behind the Laird on his horse the people stood or knelt in prayer, fearful yet with a little faltering hope, then with steadfast hope that rose to exultance as, with a terrible, choking cry that chilled the blood of all the people for a mile and more away who heard it, the loathsome worm died.

People shouted and laughed and wept for joy, crowding round their deliverer, who said: 'Och, it was just an idea I had, watching the peat on the hearth. We're well rid o' yon worm.'

They all went to the kirk, as many as could crowd in, the rest outside, to give thanks to God who had inspired the Laird.

The day and most of the night continued with celebration: feasting, singing and dancing. The news was carried to some great men and nobles, then to the King himself, who liked well to hear such exploits. The Laird was granted fertile lands to have and to hold and to pass to his heirs.

The dragon's body was, with much labour, hacked and hewed to pieces and buried deep beneath the knowe. On the green slopes the furrows long remained – they may still be there – made by the monster as he curled and coiled round the slope.

About the kirk of Linton itself there is a legend: about a hot-tempered lad and his crime, and about the brave sisters who saved him from death. The kirk is built upon sand. Now we are told in Scripture that a house built upon sand will not endure, yet the kirk has stood firm and strong.

It happened like this. A young man had murdered a priest (whether in a quarrel, in drunkenness or whatever is not told).

For this double crime, murder and sacrilege, he was condemned to death. This was agony for his two sisters who loved him dearly. They implored that he might be pardoned, declaring that he was not of evil life, and in mercy their plea was granted, but on condition that they sieve enough sand to make a firm mound on which a church could be built.

They accepted the demand and set bravely, even joyfully, to work. Patiently they sieved the sand, load after load, one relieving the other, working through day and night until a large mound, strong and firm, stood there. And on that mound the church was built and Mass said for the soul of the dead priest. Mass was said too for the soul of one of those most loving girls who from exhaustion and for joy, at the end of her task, had fallen dead.

There is a variant of this tale, told by Sir Walter Scott in his *Minstrelsy*. There were two sisters, so beautiful and desirable that, innocently or mischievously, they brought death to many wooers and rivals who fought to win them. As penance and expiation for that guilt, whether intentional or heedless, the Pope commanded them to sift the sand until they made a hillock and foundation for a kirk. And so they obeyed.

In the kirkyard was found a grave which held the bones of fifty men, and all their skulls were cleaved and broken as if by spear or sword.

Source:
William Henderson, *Notes on the Folklore of the Northern Counties of England and the Borders*

Nuckelavee

The most fearsome monster that ever haunted a countryside was Nuckelavee: an ugly name but not as ugly as the creature that bore it. He came from the sea, riding a sea-horse as fearsome as himself. Some declared that horse and rider were one, like a centaur but infinitely more horrible.

The monster's breath was poison. Fire and venom came from his mouth, destroying all that they touched, land and grass, crops and trees, leaving desolation. There was only one way of deliverance, and that was through fresh water, which he loathed: the water of a loch, a running stream and rain. He never came from the sea to the land during rain, and prayer for that must have been specially fervent, at all seasons.

He was seen by one man, Tammas, who lived to tell the tale. Tammas was coming home late one night. There was no moon but the stars shone brightly. The road, a narrow one, ran between the sea and a fresh-water loch from which a stream flowed to the sea. As Tammas walked steadily on, he heard and saw a great creature come from the sea towards him. The road was narrow, with no room to pass, and frightful as it would be to meet the creature, it would be worse to turn and flee. Pursuit was more terrifying than encounter. Tammas knew this must be Nuckelavee.

The monster was more frightful than anything he had imagined. He rode a sea-horse with fins on its legs and a mouth like a whale's, from which came that foul breath of fire and venom. The horse had one eye, as red as fire. Upon him, or part of him, sat Nuckelavee. He had no legs of his own but his arms hung down to the ground. His head was huge. Most horrible of all, he was skinless. Tammas saw the bare red flesh with black blood running through yellow veins. It was like a moment in hell.

Tammas, a brave man and good, walked on steadily. As he walked, he prayed: 'Lord, be about me, and be my defence. I am upon no evil errand. Be with me, Lord, and bring me safely to my journey's end.'

It was the Lord Himself, no doubt, Who put Tammas in mind that the creature hated and dreaded fresh water. He drew as near as he could to the loch. Nuckelavee smelled the fresh water and drew away from it towards the sea, his element; but still there was no room to pass. Tammas prayed steadily. His foot slipped into the loch, sending up a great splash of water over the forelegs of the monster's horse. The creature yelled, but Tammas rushed on, past the horror, towards the clear running stream, the blessed stream that would save him as if it were the water of baptism.

The monster turned and came after him. But it may be that the splash of loch water had weakened that great foreleg of his horse. One long arm reached out to seize Tammas and caught his bonnet – but not his head. With a great leap he crossed the blessed stream that was to him like a river in Paradise and fell on his knees to thank the Lord Who had once walked on the sea and had delivered him now. The water splashed over the evil horse and its rider. There was a terrifying roar, and Tammas turned to see Nuckelavee plunge back into the sea, it may be to death beneath the salt waves, for he was not seen again.

Source:
Sir George Douglas, *Scottish Fairy and Folk Tales* (Douglas gives as his source W. Traill Dennison in *The Scottish Antiquary*)

Brownies

Brownies

We talk of the brownies of the Borders as we might of an old
family: Scotts, Hepburns, Armstrongs, Elliots, as you will. Of
all the Other People, they belong most intimately to the
countryside. They have their history, their legend and tradition, their code of manners and behaviour which deserves
respect. Respect is indeed necessary in all dealings with the
Other People of every type and rank, whether it be a friendly
and courteous regard or a sense of awe tinged with fear. The
traditional relationship with brownies is one of mutual and
cautious friendliness.

Sir Walter Scott knew a good deal about them: 'A class of
beings distinct in habit and disposition from the freakish and
mischievous elves. . . . He was meagre, shaggy and wild in his
appearance. In the daytime he lurked in remote recesses of the
old houses which he delighted to haunt; and in the night
sedulously employed himself in discharging any laborious task
which he thought might be acceptable to the family. . . . The
Brownie does not drudge from hope of recompense. On the
contrary, so delicate is his attachment that the offer of reward
particularly of food, infallibly occasions his disappearance for
ever.'

This appears in the story of *The Brownie of Bodsbeck*. It is a
sad affair of misunderstanding, of good will gone askew. The
brownie served the family faithfully and well, until, in well-

meant gratitude, they left out a dish of bread and milk for him. He looked at it with disfavour and called out:

> Ca', Brownie, ca',
> A' the luck o' Bodsbeck's awa' to Leithenha'

– to another family who, as far as is known, kept his services.

James Hogg's novel was based on a fugitive Covenanter who lay hidden in the hills after the Battle of Bothwell Brigg. The book was regarded by many readers as a counterblast to Scott's *Old Mortality*, where the Covenanters were shown in no very favourable light. Hogg denied this, declaring that his book had been written before Scott's. But the fugitive after any rising, political or religious, may well have been the origin of an uncanny creature, lurking in hills or cave or woods by day, coming forth only at night.

With all respect both to Scott and to the tale of the Brownie of Bodsbeck, we must remember the other tradition, as familiar in England as in Scotland, which tells

> How the drudging goblin sweat
> To earn his cream bowl duly set.

The brownie liked his food. He was easily satisfied: a bowl of porridge or bread and milk was enough. But he enjoyed any small treat such as a dish of cream. What is certain is that he very properly regarded the offer of old clothes as an insult. (Brownies were not all of diminutive elfin size; some were of human height.) Aikendrum, the Brownie of Blednoch, in the poem of that name by William Nicolson, was grim of aspect but good at heart and was respected with a seemly mixture of gratitude and dread by all right-thinking people. He made his terms known. He was lured by earth and by humankind as some folk are by Elfhame and its inhabitants.

> 'I lived in a lan' where we saw nae sky,
> I dwelt in a spot where a burn rins na by;
> But I'se dwall noo wi' you if you like to try –
> Ha' ye wark for Aikendrum?

'I'll shiel a' yer sheep i' the mornin' sun,
I'll berry your crap by the licht o' the moon,
And baa the bairns wi' an unkenn'd tune
If ye'll keep puir Aikendrum.

'I'll loup the linn when ye canna wade,
I'll kirn the kirn, and I'll turn the bread,
And the wildest filly that e'er ran rede
I'se tame it', quo' Aikendrum. . . .

'I'se seek nae guids, gear, bond, nor mark,
I use nae beddin, shoon nor sark;
But a cogfu' o' brose 'tween the licht and dark
Is the wage o' Aikendrum.'

The wise old wife in the family was sure they should accept him:

Gin he do as he says – be he man, be he de'il,
Wow! we'll try this Aikendrum.

He kept his word. There was never a better worker, and

The bairnies played harmless roun' his knee,
Sae social was Aikendrum.

So all went well until

A new-made wife fu' o' frippish freaks,
Fond o' a' things feat for the first five weeks,
Laid a mouldy pair o' her ain man's breeks
By the brose o' Aikendrum.

– and that was the end.

He was heard by a herd gaun by the Threive,
Crying 'Lang, lang noo may I greet and grieve;
For alas! I ha'e gotten baith fee and leve,
O' luckless Aikendrum!'

One of the best collectors of tales, William Henderson, has maintained that the brownies were grateful for food, particularly for cream and for 'knuckled' cakes, made from meal fresh from the mill, toasted and spread with honey. The cakes should be left where they could easily be found. This kindly custom was so well known that a mother would say, when giving her child some titbit: 'There's a piece wad please a brownie.'

Henderson says also that in Berwickshire the brownie is believed to be 'the ordained helper of mankind in the drudgery entailed by sin'. Hence he is forbidden to receive wages, although he may have food and drink. He is not of the fairies, of whose origin little can be known, except that they are not of fallen humanity. There is no glamour about the brownie, either in the modern and general sense of that word or in Scott's precise definition. He is not in any way alluring. Fairies desire mortals, they allure them; they carry off human, unchristened babies and bring them to their own place of *glamour,* of illusion. Brownies may be of another world than ours, but it is very near and it is utterly apart from Elfhame. Where they live when they have no human habitation appears to be unknown.

The brownie can be mischievous and teasing, but he is not malignant. To this general statement there is one exception: in Hogg's fearsome account of 'The Brownie of the Black Haggs' – our next story to be told.

Most old families have suffered at least one disgrace, perhaps a cousin whom the decent members prefer not to know, and the brownies have one in the creature called Red Cap, Red Comb or Bloody Comb, who haunts old castles and towers where evil has been done. He himself is evil in wish and intent, antagonistic to the good. He likes to terrify. The decent brownies may be ugly, but it is in a homely, even a comic way. Red Cap is hideous and menacing, with red eyes, long teeth and talons for nails. He wears iron shoes and carries a pike-staff, all for the malignant purpose of terrifying mortals whom he may meet. He lurks in the dark, ready to attack late and lonely travellers, at whom he throws stones. He collects their blood in his cap; hence his name. Human strength is of small help against him, but this unholy creature can be driven off by holy weapons: the sign of the cross, some words of Holy Writ, the utterance of the Name of God.

But the brownie's real function and nature is to help or, by way of diversion, to tease, sometimes with the excuse of giving a moral lesson. He can keep a strict eye upon careless servants and pounce upon any who lapse. This happened in a house where the mistress was stingy with the food. Her two young maids had healthy appetites, always hungry, never satisfied. One day they decided to help themselves. One brought a bowl of milk from the dairy, the other a bannock from the larder. They sat down by the kitchen fire with the bowl between them, broke the bannock in half and ate and drank, passing the bowl from one to the other. One can hardly blame them, but the brownie did. He came between them, invisible, reached for the bowl of milk and drank heartily.

'Ye've ta'en mair than yer share,' said one girl.

'I've dune neathing o' the sort. It's yersel' that has drunk owre much.'

There was a hoarse chuckle and a hoarse voice spoke: 'It's neither ane nor tither. It's mysel' that has drunk the milk, ha, ha, ha! That'll teach ye no' to steal.'

Perhaps it did. But we could wish that he had taught the grudging mistress a lesson too.

One of the most serviceable of brownies was the guardian, as Scott tells us, of a family near Jedburgh. The lady of the house was brought to premature labour, and a servant was told to ride at once to the town to bring a midwife. He was a slack fellow, who was so long in getting himself and his horse ready that the good brownie lost patience, dressed himself in the man's riding coat, saddled the best horse in the stable and rode off like the wind. He found the midwife and took her up behind him.

Meanwhile the Tweed had risen high. That was no obstacle to this intrepid rider, who plunged in without heed for the midwife or for his horse and came safely across and on to the house, where the nurse was just in time to deliver the child and make the mother comfortable. Meanwhile the brownie, finding the servant only beginning to draw on his boots, gave him a sound thrashing.

The gratitude of the laird and his lady was profound. What could they give this faithful creature as reward? It would seem that they had heard him wish for a green coat, so, forgetful of the old tradition that one must not give any clothes to a brownie, they left out for him a braw new coat of fairy green. He was not offended, but the gift appealed to the fairy blood in him, rousing memories or desire, and he departed for ever, to dwell with those Other People.

The late Katherine Briggs, a distinguished scholar of our own time who knew more about the Other People than most, tells in her story of 'Hobbledy Dick' how that good creature served a family faithfully and well through many years, and how a young husband and wife, not in ignorance or ingratitude or folly but in true gratitude, provided him with a choice of coats. They realized that he might now long to return to his own country. One coat was red, the colour of warm, human blood, the other of the fairy green. No word was spoken, but Hobbledy Dick assumed the green coat and, with thankfulness in his faithful heart, went to his own people, his long service discharged and rewarded. Scott would have liked that tale.

Source:
Sir George Douglas, *Scottish Fairy and Folk Tales*

The Brownie of the Black Haggs

Brownies are for the most part decent folk, doing no one any harm if no one harms them, doing in fact a great deal of good, helping about the house by night, a blessing to good house-wives. But the brownie of the Black Haggs was very different, and so was the housewife whom he visited. She was far from good; her name was much detested in the countryside. Folk did not hesitate to accuse her of witchcraft, though not openly.

The family was that of the Sprots of Wheelhope, an old family, now sadly diminished. The old Laird and his wife had only one son, a child and not over strong. The Laird had been late in marrying and had married neither wisely nor well. He was a decent man enough, but of no great ability, and was now rather doddering.

His lady was heartily detested for her vile-tempered cruelty towards her servants when angered. Any slight fault on their part brought abuse and blows, and once even worse, for she had been so enraged at one poor girl that she had struck her to the ground, and the girl died of the blow. That caused talk and scandal enough, and there was more when another maid died suddenly, without illness. Poison was suspected. She was a bonny lass, and it may be that the Laird had looked at her with more favour than his lady approved, for, little as she cared for him, she would tolerate no straying of his duty, some might call it his subservience to her. When the poor maid was buried, he stood at the graveside, wiping his eyes: 'Puir lass, puir lass. I wish she hadna got something she died of.'

The only person for whom Mrs Sprot (or Lady Wheelhope as she was usually called) had any affection was her son, whom indeed it would have been difficult not to love. His father loved him dearly. He was a handsome boy, quick and clever of mind, friendly in manner, and the whole household were very fond of him.

After the death of a second maid, the mutterings grew. Some of the neighbours took their suspicions to the sheriff, and there was an enquiry, but nothing came of it, and the matter was dropped. For a time the lady kept quiet and did no harm.

Then a new servant came to the household who called himself Merodach. He was a very strange-looking fellow, very dark of face, almost uncannily quick in movement. There was indeed something uncanny about his whole appearance. Sometimes his face was that of an old man, yet his movements were those of youth, and he was stronger than any of the other men or lads, and he worked well.

His fellow-servants could make little of him. He rarely spoke, and he did not sit with them or hang about the yard. He ate and drank very sparingly, never sitting long at table, but he was always civil to the others, always willing to do any job. If he chose to keep himself aloof, that was his own affair, and he was left in peace.

But the mistress hated him as she had never hated anyone before, and he returned her hatred. This was quite obvious to everyone. She did all she could to plague him, and for that she had a great capacity. It would have driven anyone else crazy or sent them hurrying away from the place, but this fellow only laughed and provoked her to more and more rages. Once she rushed at him to strike him, but she was heavy and awkward in her movements and he was quick as a cat or a monkey. He dodged her, and in her rush she knocked down a decent fellow, one John Thomson, with whom she herself was on good terms. He struck his head on the floor and was long in coming to. In a new frenzy she threw the heavy kitchen poker at Merodach, who dodged that too. It struck the dresser, smashing the plates and jugs on the shelves. The mistress complained to the Laird, declaring that Merodach had struck and felled John Thomson, then hurled the poker.

'What ails ye at decent John Thomson?' the Laird asked him. 'And what garred ye break a' the delf on the dresser?'

'I did neither t'ane nor t'ither,' Merodach told him. 'It was the mistress hersel'.'

The other servants declared that he spoke the truth. He had never shown any violence to any of them. The Laird was sorely troubled, for he had no fault to find with Merodach, and he could not forget those poor girls who had died.

Merodach ate and drank very little. He lived on bread and milk and had stipulated a very moderate amount of those daily. The mistress had a spiteful pleasure in delaying his supply, in reducing it. Then one morning she set on the table a large bowl of new creamy milk to which she had added a dose of deadly poison. Merodach came into the kitchen. The lady stood watching. Her little son ran in, followed by her spaniel, Missie, the only other creature for whom she had any affection. Merodach stood looking at them and at the bowl of milk on the table. The boy was chattering and held his mother's attention, while Merodach spoke to the dog: 'Here, wee Missie; ye're hungry. See if ye like my breakfast.'

He set the bowl of milk on the floor, and the spaniel lapped it up eagerly, wagging her tail. The mistress turned, and when she saw what was happening, she gave a wild shriek and rushed to pick up the dog. The poor little creature stiffened in her arms and died within a few moments. She ran out of the kitchen into the yard, followed by her little son and one or two servants. They found her frantically digging a grave for the dog, with her hands.

She wept and lamented wildly, cursing Merodach all the time. The little boy was terrified and ran back into the house. The servants muttered. Merodach came out and looked at the tiny body lying in its shallow grave:

'Eh, the puir we cratur. Wha did this? Wha put the poison in the bowl of milk?'

This drove the woman to the verge of madness. She cursed Merodach as she had never cursed before. He laughed. 'It has come upon yer ain heid.'

The poor old Laird was nearly demented, but far worse yet
lay in store for him. Next morning his little son was found
dead, murdered in his bed, strangled and covered with blood.
On the lady's hands and clothes there were bloodstains, for at
last she had crossed the border of madness. The Laird was
helpless, unable either to act or to speak. One of the servants
went to report to the sheriff, who came to the house, accompanied by the lady's brother, also a man of the law. They made a
most careful investigation, questioning all the servants, including Merodach. They found no scrap of evidence against any of
them, for they were all profoundly shocked and grieved. It
became horribly clear who was guilty. The plan of the ramb-
ling old house gave a clue.

The boy shared a room with his tutor, who slept in a bed by
the door, while the boy's bed lay by the opposite wall. Above
that room was one shared by Merodach and another servant,
and Merodach's bed was by the wall opposite the door. It soon
became painfully clear that, in her mad hatred of Merodach,
the woman had determined to kill him; distracted by her own
evil frenzy, she had gone into the wrong room, towards the
inner wall, seized and murdered her own son.

The child was laid in his grave. His father, poor fellow, was
by this time quite out of his mind. Merodach stayed no longer
in the fateful house. He was not guilty, but he left behind him a
trail of rumour. Was he human? Had he come from some
far-off land? Was he a warlock or a brownie? Someone called
him 'the brownie of the Black Haggs'.

The mistress herself disappeared. There was a search for her,
but it was not likely that she would be found or that the reward
offered for finding her would be claimed.

The Laird's old shepherd, Wattie Blyth, was told of this
when he came down from his herding on the hill. His wife told
him she was sure that Merodach, the brownie, was still about
the place, for his spirit hung like a dark cloud or mist.

'It's the Ither People who ha'e her. They ken Merodach weel,
he is ane of them. They care nocht for ony reward. They'll
haud her. Find Merodach and ye'll find her.'

'So that's the wey o't. I'll no say ye're wrang,' said Wattie.
'She's been ripe for destruction this mony a day. She aye made

a mock o' religion, and nae gude can come to them that dae that. It's the end o' the Sprots o' Wheelhope. A wumman like that is a curse.'

'Ye're richt, Wattie. Noo, keep ye a gled e'e for him or for her. There's mony an uncanny place about here, mony a neuk amang the hills. She may be held by yon Ither Folk, but should ye come on her or ony trace o' her, there'd be a gude reward.'

Wattie stood considering. 'That reminds me, I heard a fearsome skirl this morning about the Brockholes, no unlike her leddyship in any o' her rages, but waur than ony I ever heard: a skreich o' dread, a kind o' chokin'. I'm thinkin' I'd better gae up that wey. But heaven forgi'e me, I'm feart.'

At that moment there was a terrifying noise at the door. The shepherd went to open it and cried out: 'It's themsel's: hersel' and the brownie. He hauds her by the hair o' her heid, and he is beatin' her sair wi' a muckle stick, as I wadna beat a brute beast. Gude protect us!'

Wattie took his Bible from the shelf and opened it to find counsel. Merodach appeared, aged in look beyond that of the oldest man they had ever seen, appallingly grim of aspect, dragging the woman, who was bruised and cut and bleeding, her clothing in rags.

'Put awa' that buik,' he ordered.

'I'll no' dae that for you or onyone,' declared Wattie.

'Put it aside and hearken to me. Syne ye can read it as ye please. An' tak this wumman back whaur she belangs, and lat them that are luikin' for her dae what they wull. She is a plague to me. I'll ha'e nocht mair to do wi' her. I maun awa' to my ain place.'

He threw the wretched creature on the floor and went out, crashing the door behind him. Wattie and his wife raised the woman. They tried to bind her arms, to hold her, but she broke away and ran out after Merodach. He turned and felled her with one blow. Wattie and his wife bound her then, lifted her and staggered away with her to the house where the doddering old Laird sat with his brother-in-law. He gave them scant welcome, you can be sure.

'What for dae ye bring her here? I'll ha'e nocht to do wi' her. Better she had died oot there. Tak' her awa'.'

The brother-in-law, however, received them well. He thanked them for what they had done, when he had heard their tale. The woman was carried to her room and was well guarded. She lay long unconscious.

The brother and the sheriff agreed that Wattie and his wife had earned the reward. The Laird was quite indifferent. But although she was well guarded, the lady disappeared again. She was found among some black peat haggs on the hill, and her dead body was a fearsome sight. The brownie was never seen again, but his name and legend were not forgotten. The old Laird died, babbling and mindless. And that was the end of the Sprots of Wheelhope.

Source:
James Hogg, *The Ettrick Shepherd's Tales*

Ghosts and Hauntings

The Phantom Bride

I'm the Laird o' Windywa's,
I camena here without a cause,
And I ha'e gotten forty fa's
In coming owre the knowe, joe;
The nicht it is baith wind and weet.
The morn it will be snaw and sleet;
My shoon are frozen to my feet;
O, rise and let me in, joe.
Let me in this a'e nicht.

So Allan Sandison, the young Laird of Birkendelly, sang as he rode on his way from Birkendelly to 'the muckle toun', as it was called, of Balmawhapple. It was 9 August, the Eve of St Laurence. He rode carelessly, sang hilariously, with never a serious thought in his head until suddenly, on the road before him, he saw the most lovely girl walking swiftly and gracefully. She wore a white gown with a green cloak and veil. Allan, though still unattached, had an eye for pretty girls and a way with them and thought he knew all those in the neighbourhood; but he had never seen this girl before, and her beauty was beyond any he had set eyes on.

How had she so suddenly appeared? There was no wood or thicket on that part of the road. Now she seemed to walk more slowly, almost as if she were waiting for him.

'I'll soon overtake you, my bonny lass,' he thought, and put his horse to a canter. But he could not come up with the lady, who vanished as suddenly as she had appeared. Yet there was no hiding-place on the road. Allan rode faster but still had no glisk of her. He was no longer singing, nor did he feel hilarious any longer, for a strange chill clutched his heart.

'Och, but she's bonny. I maun see her face to face and ha'e a word with her. She canna be far away. I'll ride up the hill.'

But when he came to the top of Birkybrow, there was no sign of her. Instead he met a neighbour, one MacMurdie, riding doucely along.

'Whaur awa, Birkendelly?' he called. 'Ridin' as if the dei'l were after you?'

'Have you seen a lady, a bonny lass she is, dressed in green and white? She was on the road, walking gey fast; then awa' out o' sight and whar could she hide here? Whaur is she?'

'Ye're daft, laddie, daft or dreamin',' said MacMurdie in a kind, indulgent voice. 'There's been naebody on the road, neither lass nor loon, young nor auld since I cam' along.' Allan stared at him, bewildered, shivering a little. 'Come alang wi' me, laddie. I'm riding doun tae the mill, syne I'll turn and ride hame. We'll see if there's ony leddy on the road.'

Allan turned his horse and rode back to the mill with MacMurdie, who dealt quickly with his business there, then they rode together towards Birkybrow.

'There she is,' Birkendelly cried suddenly. 'Look – in her white gown and green cloak and veil. Faith, but she's bonny.'

'Laddie, ye're clean daft,' said MacMurdie. 'I see no leddy, and my sicht's gey clear. Ye're seein' the green o' the leaves in the sun.'

Allan paid no heed. He spurred his horse on, then stopped. The lady had vanished, like a mist, like a shadow, like a phantom. He rode on slowly. Something made him wheel his horse round. There she was again, clear in the sun, in her white and green.

'Wait! Bide for me! I'm coming,' he called, and the lady appeared to walk more slowly while Allan rode faster. Then once more she vanished.

Poor young Birkendelly rode slowly on. By this time Mac-Murdie had gone off by himself. Allan rode, as he had set out to do, towards the muckle toun of Balmawhapple where there was a stir of life, people in the streets going about their business, stopping to talk, drifting into the inn for a dram. Allan followed there, sat down and ordered a brandy. Whatever business had brought him to the town in the first place, he had now forgotten. Presently MacMurdie came in, greeting everyone; he sat down beside Allan, looking at him quizzically but kindly and with a touch of concern.

'What ails ye, lad? There's an unco luik about your face, a kind o' flush.'

Allan laughed, without much mirth. 'Sit ye doun, MacMurdie, and drink with me.'

MacMurdie obeyed but still looked concerned. 'Maybe ye'd better see a doctor, lad. Ye mind me o' a friend o' mine – who kept seein' a young officer, in an auld uniform that hadna been worn for a hundred years or mair. That showed he wasna real. My friend had a gude doctor, who sent him to bed, bled him, gi'ed him a soothing draught, kept him on a low diet. He slept a lang time, twal' hours or mair, and woke wi' his mind clear, himsel' again. There was never another glisk o' the young officer.'

Allan smiled faintly. The advice was good, but he took no action. MacMurdie, a kindly man, asked him to stay for a few days with him and his good wife. She was as kind as her husband. They were a cheerful, hospitable couple, with lively but well-behaved bairns. People liked coming to their house; it was a tonic to be there. Allan walked and rode with his host and was pleasant with all who came to the house, but there was something withdrawn about him, silent; he was no longer the exuberant young man most people knew. Some of the older folk shook their heads.

Allan was the only son of his father, who had died a few years before. He had one sister who now lived in Ireland. She had married the son and heir of a squire called O'Brien. Allan was persuaded to pay her a visit, which indeed he did willingly. They had always been devoted to each other, and he liked his brother-in-law very well. Now young Captain O'Brien was also an only son, but he had seven sisters, all younger than himself, and his wife was benevolently determined to find good husbands for them in turn. They were charming girls, especial-

ly the eldest, Lina, who she thought would make a perfect wife
for Allan. On a previous visit, the young laird had appeared to
agree, although he had not come to the point of proposing.
Now, surely, it would reach that happy climax.

On this visit, however, Allan was singularly quiet. He was
always pleasant in manner, friendly, attentive to Lina, but no
more than that. When his sister spoke, as she did discreetly, of
Lina's many qualities, he agreed. She was very pretty, amiable
and gifted: a good housewife, a graceful dancer, musical,
singing her own Irish songs to the harp, and Allan had an ear
and a taste for music. What more could a man want?

There was a fine ball at the Big House, given by Squire
O'Brien and his wife, and there were smaller parties at the
cottage or dower house where the young O'Briens lived. Allan
took part, but there was a strange new quietness about him, a
remoteness which puzzled his sister. He danced at the parties,
he listened to Lina's singing, he even sang himself some of the
old songs he had loved since childhood, but nothing more
happened.

One warm evening Lina was walking in the grounds of the
Big House. She was wearing a white muslin frock with a green
cloak thrown round her shoulders. Allan saw her and came
running towards her, crying out: 'Wait for me, oh wait!' –
which she very willingly did, turning towards him with a smile.
Suddenly he stopped, the look of expectancy on his face fading
into bewilderment. 'Lina, forgive me. I thought – heaven help
me!' He turned and walked away, his head and shoulders
bowed.

Early on the following evening he was coming back from
fishing when he again saw a girl in white, with a green cloak.
'Lina,' he thought. 'I was boorish towards her yestereen, I must
make my apologies and my peace with her.'

He hastened forward, calling out in a friendly voice. The
lady turned and looked at him. It was not Lina. It was the
vision he had first seen by Birkybrow. She did not walk
towards him, but she did not walk away either; she stood very
still, looking at him, and her face and eyes were the loveliest
that he had ever seen.

'My lady, my love. At last we meet! Now may I take you to

my sister's house? She will receive you with kindness and joy. My love, let us be married soon.'

The lady stood there, unchanged, but the surroundings changed suddenly and dramatically. He was no longer on O'Brien's land but on his own land at Birkybrow where he had first seen her, the elusive, lovely lady. Now she spoke, in a voice like far-off music, yet very clear.

'I have come, but it is not yet time for our wedding. I shall come again on the Eve of St Laurence to be your bride. My name is Jane Ogilvie. You know me only now, but I have long known your family. Now let us exchange rings.'

They were standing close to each other. She leaned over and kissed him, and he was transported with joy. Allan drew from his finger the gold signet ring with which his father and grandfather and great-grandfather had betrothed their brides; he placed it on the lady's finger, and in return she gave him one set with a great emerald, green as grass, but strangely tinged with a flush of red, like blood. Suddenly a dense white mist overwhelmed him, and the lady vanished. He could visualize her so clearly that he almost seemed to hear her voice, and yet there was no sign of her. The mist swirled, and he was no longer in his own Borderland but on the O'Brien land, not far from the Big House and his sister's cottage.

He was like a man in a dream. Somehow his body took over, and he walked back to the cottage, handed over the fish he had caught and had supper with the family. It was not the first time on that visit that he had seemed silent and withdrawn, and he hardly remembered finding his way to bed.

Now one of the most important and respected members of the household was his sister's old nurse, Luckie Black. She had been nurse to their mother before them. Their mother had died young when they were quite small bairns, and Luckie had mothered them through their childhood. It had been a sore difficulty for her, when her girl married, to decide whether to go with her to Ireland or stay with Master Allan, for the Laird their father was dead by that time. In the end Luckie Black chose to go. A marriage is likely to produce babies, and she longed to have children to look after again. Master Allan showed no signs of being married or even betrothed. She had been happy there with bairns to cherish and admonish, and now she thought that possibly Allan would marry Miss Lina, and they might ask her to go with them to Birkendelly and look after the next generation.

Next morning Allan rose and dressed and joined the family where they were often to be found, in Luckie's room. She sat there, very straight and upright, in her black gown and white cap and ruffles. On a table beside her lay her Bible and Thomas Beston's *Fourfold Estate*. Allan greeted her affectionately as usual, then announced rather abruptly that he must soon be leaving. He must be home before the Eve of St Laurence.

'Gude save us, what's that ye say? Ye maunna say that, you maunna dae that,' cried the old woman. Then she saw on his hand the ring with its great emerald, flushed with blood-red. She rose with a cry, seized his hand, tried to draw off the ring and fell into a swoon.

She was lifted tenderly and carried to her bed. They sent for the doctor, but he could do nothing to revive her. All that day she lay motionless, her eyes open but unseeing; she moaned a little but spoke no word. In the night she died. They all mourned for her who had been so faithful, so loving and so well loved.

On the day after her funeral Allan told his sister he must return home at once. He had shown no emotion about his old nurse, and this grieved his sister almost as much as their parting.

There was a great welcome at Birkendelly for the young Laird, from friends and neighbours and all the folk on the estate. He was gentle and courteous with everyone but strangely remote. He bade his housekeeper prepare the great bed-chamber, the bridal room of the family; he ordered a fine new suit from his tailor. Naturally his friends and his tenants could not help wondering whom he would bring home as his bride.

On the Eve of St Laurence Allan rode out. He took no groomsman with him; he asked no lady to attend his bride. The house was all ready, and the faithful MacMurdie came to await Allan's return, and with him the minister, although no banns had been read.

Allan rode his horse up Birkybrow. He was seen by more

than one, riding with a lady on the croup behind him, a lady dressed in bridal white and fairy green.

He did not come back to his house, but his horse came, riderless, in a frenzied gallop. They found Allan lying on Birkybrow, dead, grievously bruised, his face livid and distorted with terror. Of the lady there was no trace at all. They brought the young Laird home and prepared him for burial with his fathers. On the table in his room lay a letter addressed to his sister.

'Dearest sister,

By this time tomrrow I shall be either the happiest or most miserable of men. I go tonight to meet the loveliest of ladies, Jane Ogilvie, whom I have met before and whom I met again on your land. There we exchanged rings and plighted our troth. It may be a far journey till I come home again – it may be long before I see you.

Yours, with love till death,

Allan.'

For his family and friends grief was mingled unbearably with bewilderment, almost with terror. What had happened? What had possessed Allan? Who was this Jane Ogilvie whose name no one knew? Some of the older people had dim memories of something heard long ago, but none was clear.

Then late in the year a very old woman, Peg, came back to this countryside where she had been born and lived in her childhood. As a young girl she had gone off with a tinker husband and lived with him wherever he went. Now that he was dead, she came back to the place where she had been brought up. Inevitably she heard the tale, and her memories revived. She went to the minister to tell him all she knew of the tale she had heard in childhood from father and grandfather.

Long ago the Laird of Birkendelly, Allan's great-great grandfather, had been betrothed to a lady, Jane Ogilvie, who was beautiful and who loved him but who had a very small tocher. The Laird was in need of money, so when he met a rich heiress, he threw over Jane Ogilvie to marry this wealthy bride. On the Eve of St Laurence he had ridden out towards Birkybrow and never returned. His horse had come back to the stable, galloping quickly. His body had been found, bruised and broken, his face distorted.

Old Peg had come one day, in her childhood, to a lonely grave where red blood stained the green turf. When she ran home in terror, her grandfather bade her never speak of it. Later she heard him and her father talk, and heard the tale she now told the minister.

'I've keepit silence till noo, but I've heard the tale o' the young Laird and the leddy he saw. It has aye been an uncanny place up by Birkybrow. My auld grandfaither and my faither too kenned mair than they ever tauld. Aye, there was mony a word, low-spoken, when I was a bairn, aboot the bonny Jane Ogilvie. Maybe the wierd has been dreed at last.'

The minister prayed with her, and bade her now keep the tale to herself.

'And may God have mercy on the soul of that poor lady, and on him who betrayed her, and on our young Laird.'

There was no sign of blood on Allan's green grave. But there was never again a Sandison at Birkendelly.

Source:
James Hogg, *The Ettrick Shepherd's Tales*

The Ghost with the Golden Casket

This tale was told by an old man, Will Borlan, to a young English visitor. The setting was on the western Borders, above the Solway, in sight of Caerlaverock Castle. The young man was sitting on a green grass mound in the derelict garden of a deserted cottage. The old man came leading a cow.

'Na, na, my bonny lass, ye maunna graze here,' he told the cow, who wanted to stop and feed on the lush green grass of the old garden. 'This is cursed ground. If you feed here, your milk and butter will bring sickness and ill luck to my ain gran-children and to a' wha taste them. Com on, noo, lass.'

He drew her firmly onto other pasture, where he sat down on a knoll, then looked at the stranger in the old garden. They greeted each other courteously, and the old man said: 'Sir, I counsel ye, dinna sit there. It'll bring you ill luck. Nane here wad let their cattle graze or their bairns play there, for an ill story hings aboot the place. Come ye here, and sit by me.' The young man rose and joined him. 'Ye're a stranger to these pairts, and I'm thinkin' ye're English.'

'Partly,' the young fellow replied, 'but I had a Scots grand-mother whom I loved dearly and who came from this very part.'

'And wha was she?'

'Her name was Marion Scobie, and she married my grand-father and went with him over the Border; but she never forgot her birthplace, and she spoke with a Scots tongue and taught me many a good Scots word.'

'So ye're the grandson o' bonny Marion Scobie; I loo'ed her weel. She should ha'e become Marion Borland – I'm Will Borland – but there; she loo'ed her English bridegroom better than me. I can see a luik of her in your face, in your een. And sae, while we sit here, I'll tell you the tale o' this ruined cottage and of what cam' to its owner, the fisherman Gilbert Gyrape, and the Ghost with the Gowden Casket.' This is his tale.

'It is fifty years and mair since a gude ship was wrecked, doun there in the Solway, on a nicht o' storm, thunder and lightning, rain and hail and squalls o' wind. The foam lay as thick and white as the snaw on the roof of Caerlaverock Castle. My faither stood at the door, luikin' oot. "Dule and wae for them that sail the firth this nicht. God keep them."

'He saw a ship come towards the shore, her canvas torn, her mast broken, the sea foaming owre her. I stood there wi' my faither, and as he spoke a flash of lightning showed us two people, man and woman, both richly dressed, the leddy with a flash o' jewels aboot her, staun' on the deck, haudin' close tae each ither.

'"Saddle me my black horse and saddle me my grey," my faither orders. "An' bring them doun tae Deid Man's Bank. We'll ha'e need o' them to save thae puir folk."

'I brocht the horses but they werena needit. Afore we could ride, a great wave swept owre the doomed ship. The bonny couple were doun, doun amang the waves. We ran doun to the shore, an' there we met the fisherman Gilbert Gyrape, that had this cottage.

'"I've tried to save them, the leddy an' her husband, but there were swept awa'. I've dune my best."

'"Gin ye truly tried to save them," said my faither. "Ye'll ha'e yer reward hereafter; but if ye cared mair for the gowd and jewels that puir leddy wore, then dule an' doom will come upon ye."

'E'en as he spak, we were doun at the watter's edge, and a great wave washed ashore the leddy's body. My faither lifted her gently and he saw that jewels had been torn frae her ears, rings frae her fingers, a necklace frae her neck. It was nae sea that had dune that, though the sea had drouned her; there were marks on her neck and briest, her fingers were bruised, her ears torn. The puir leddy was buried wi' sorrow and reverence in the kirkyaird; her husband's body was never washed up. Nane frae that wreck was saved. My faither said nae mair. He never accused Gilbert to his face of having dune this thing, but he never spak word to him again, nor took his haun or broke bried wi' him or sat si' him by the hearth.

'At first Gilbert prospered exceedingly. He merriet and had children; he gave up this cottage and had a fine new hoose built. He joined a godly sect and had hard words and sour looks for puir folk that went a thocht astray. He won power and riches, but he had no respect. Few wad tak' him by the haun' or gang to his hoose or bid him to theirs. The verra beggars wouldna ask frae him.

'It is an uncanny tale I ha'e to tell ye noo. I'd gane doun ae nicht, wi' my faither to the shore. We were luikin' at oor nets. The sea was still, there was nae wind, the sky was clear. Suddenly we heard a sound as the wings owre the water, and a licht shine, a line o' licht, dancin' and glimmerin' owre the water, a licht neither o' moon nor stars.

'"God keep us in His hauns," said my faither.

'The licht moved up owre the shore and into Gilbert's cottage, empty as we thocht since he left for his fine new hoose. There was a skriech o' fear, and three men cam' rushin' oot whom we kent as three o' the maist notorious smugglers on the coast. They cam' rinnin' doun tae us.

'"That's the maist fearsome sicht e'er I saw," said ane. "It's a warnin', and I'll hae nae mair o' this trede we follow. I'll bide at hame and repent o' my sins."

'"I'll speir nocht aboot your trede," says my faither, "but ye'll dae weel to repent. What ha'e ye seen and heard?"

'"I ha'e seen mony a fearsome thing at sea, but yon licht that cam' into the cottage was mair awesome than ony. What it is sent for I daurna think. Gude forgi'e me."

'"An' forbye," added a second man, "I saw a ghaist: a leddy in white stood within that licht. She was haudin' a gowden casket close to her, as if tae keep it from bein' ta'en; and there were marks on her neck and briest."

'The third man said: "Let's awa', noo, and tak' oor kegs o'

brandy to the Baillie and the laird, an' never bring sic a cargo ashore again."

'My faither spak gude words to the men, tellin' them he had seen the uncanny licht himsel'. There was nae licht to be seen at the cottage windows. The three went in, cam' oot wi' the kegs, loaded their boat and rowed awa'.

'The tale spread – no by my faither, but ithers had seen the uncanny licht, and mony remembered that shipwreck. It lost nocht in the tellin'. Some saw the licht, some vowed they had had a glisk o' the leddy in white. Then ae winter nicht douce Davie Haining was ridin' hame frae the Rood Fair at Dumfries. It was mirk, mirk and quaiet – till he heard horses' hooves ahint him and a rider cam' up wi' him and passed him, fleein' wi' a skriech o' terror. It was gey like Gilbert Gyrape. Ahint and abune reachin' for him was a shadow, a ghaist or phantom, fair fearsome tae see. The rider rushed on, and Davie rode hame, wi' a prayer in his he'rt. Frae that nicht nocht went weel wi' Gilbert. His crops withered in the fields, his flocks de'ed. His wife and his bairns, ane by ane, sickened and de'ed. Nae servants wad wark in his hoose, and ae nicht it took fire and was burned to the ground. Sinsyne he hes dwalt his lane, in the auld cottage there. He maun be mair than fower-score.'

Old Will paused, and the young fellow sat silent. 'Luik, there he comes,' said Will.

The door of the cottage opened and an old man came out, bent and frail, hobbling on a stick. He wore an old, worn-out coat, his shoes hardly held on his feet. His hair and beard were long and unkempt, his face thin and worn and wrinkled. On his head he wore a fisherman's cap.

Feebly he stumbled towards the shore and the sea, then made a sudden rush to the water's edge, crying out: 'Bonny leddy, bonny leddy, gi'e me yer gowden casket. Na, na, dinna haud oot a haun' in pleadin'. Ye ha'e owre mony bonny jewels.'

He waded into the water, held his own hands beneath as if clutching something and brought them out as if holding something, muttering: 'Eh the bonny diamonds, the bonny gowden necklace, the gowden casket. She's gane now; I'll ha'e gowd and gear and lands. I'll be a laird and a power in the land. May the sea haud her and keep her.'

The young man and Will rose together and went quickly down to the shore.

'Come ye back, Gilbert,' called old Will. But even as he called, as the two ran down to the shore, a huge wave surged in and swept the feeble old Gilbert down, down and under the water that had drowned a bonny lady years before, a lady robbed and killed for her jewels.

'God forgi'e him,' said old Will, and the young man said 'Amen'. 'And may the puir leddy rest noo, and ne'er come back to haunt us.'

And so ended the story of 'The Ghost with the Golden Casket'.

Source:
Allan Cunningham, *Traditional Tales of the English and Scottish Peasantry*

The Haunted Ships

Two young men were in their boat on the Solway. It was a clear, starlit evening. There was a roll on the water, which made it clear to the fishermen that there were salmon for the catching.

An old man came wandering down from one of the cottages above the shore, carrying a net on his back, and with him walked a girl with a harpoon, and they sat down together on a rock.

One of the young men, born and bred on that coast, whispered to the other: 'That's old Mark MacMoran and his granddaughter, Barbara. He knows every inch of the shore and the sea. He has seen and heard more than most folk – and not all of it canny. He has seen the haunted ships; there may well be a bit of a warlock in him.'

'Would he tell us anything?' asked the second youth.

'Maybe; it depends on his mood. Let's pull the boat ashore. We'd be better on land for a while. The tide's rising and this is a bad bit of coast.'

The two jumped out, drew their boat up and walked towards old Mark MacMoran and his granddaughter, a bonny lass. Old Mark was looking at two black hulls of ships, nearly sunk in the quicksands, almost submerged by the tide. Even as they walked up to him, the water rushed over those black uncanny hulls, and no more was seen of the drowned ships.

'Blessed be the tide that covers ye, more blessed still when it covers ye for ever, ye cursed ships. May it sweep ye awa' for ever, doun, doun in the deeps. Ye were sailed here to do evil, evil befell ye, evil ha'e ye dune ever since. Cursed be the land where the trees grew that made ye, cursed be the axe that shaped ye, the water where ye were launched, and the wind that brocht ye here. Ye ha'e ta'en three sons frae me. I ken ye're fain to get me mysel'. Aye, ye're after a victim the nicht, but it'll no' be me.'

As they sat there, a young fisherman came down from the cottage, carrying his net and a spear. He greeted the group and walked down and into the rough water.

'Come back, ye young fule,' Mark shouted, rising to his feet and waving his arms. 'Come back, I bid ye; ye kenna what that tide can do.'

'Come back, come back,' the girl cried, beginning to sob, holding out her arms. But the salmon were rising, and the young fisherman was heedless, for he saw only the chance of a fine catch. 'The tide will catch ye,' cried the girl, and the tide caught him indeed, sweeping him down into the deep.

'Aye, ye've gotten a victim now,' said old Mark, while the girl cried bitterly. The two young men leapt to their feet and rushed to their boat, pushing off and trying to save the fisherman. But there was never a sign of him.

'It's of no avail,' old Mark told them grimly when they came sadly back. 'The ships will suffer nane to gae near them, nane to touch them, an' he touched a rib o' ane o' the hulls, touched and tried to haud it.'

'Aye, he was doomed frae that moment,' cried an old woman who had come down to the rocks. 'Nane could save him; his doom cam' upon him.'

'Aye, and it's lucky the twa o' ye didna follow him,' Mark told the young men.

They all sat for a few minutes in silence, thinking of the victim. Then one of the young men said to Mark: 'Tell us more about those dreadful ships.'

'They cam' frae Denmark lang, lang syne. The ships they ha'e wrecked are deep beneath the water, rotted awa'; but whiles, as noo, the black hulls o' the haunted ships are to be

seen, an' they are to da'e herm. They were sent to work havoc
on our shores. They cam' on a nicht o' the harvest moon. The
reapers had worked late, the hairst was gethered into the
bonny gowden sheaves, and the men cam' doun tae the shore.
They saw two ships come sailin' in. The first had neither
captain nor crew aboard but only a shape, a black shadow
flichterin' aboot the deck, appearin' to rig the sails, to steer the
ship. The ither had captain, mate and crew and ither folk
forbye. There was the soun o' music and laughter, neither o'
them canny. The tide was sweeping in, high and strang. The
reapers shouted to the crew to sail carefully, but nane tak'd
heed but a muckle black dog at the prow, that answered wi' a
howl.

'"It's the fiend himsel' in a bottomless ship," said ane o' the
reapers, an auld, wyse man. "We maun pray."

'"Hoots, it's juist auld Janet Withershins and her cummers
haudin their revels," said a young man. "Fine I'd like to be
amang them. There will be a spate o' gude red wine, nane o' yer
wersh stuff, byt wine that warms the he'rt's blude, wine that
gars ye lowp and dance, that wad raise a newly-steekit
corpse."

'"Aye," agreed another lad. "It'll be nane o' yer fairy wine
either, that some tell o', which is nae drink at a'. I had a drink
o't aince frae auld Marion Mathers, her that was said to be a
witch. Whan she deed they wad hae buried her in the auld
kirkyaird whaur nane had been buried for mony a year, but she
raise frae the grave, and they had to lay her in the new
kirkyaird up yonder, among ither folk. Fegs, but it was graun'
wine she gi'ed me. I'd risk a droukin' noo for a cup o' the
same."

'"An' sae wad I," agreed the first lad.

'"Bide a wee, ye puir fules an' sinners," said a third, and he
was the son o' a minister that had little divinity, and o' his wife
that had a muckle thirst for the liquor. "These ships are truly
driven by the fiend, and they will come to wreck, and a' aboard
will be drouned. Then we can gang to the wreckage. There
will be barrels o' wine, kegs o' brandy. We can tak' a' we
want."

'Then, as if he had heard (and mebbe he had) the black

shadow on the first ship stopped both ships, lat doun a black boat wi' shadowy rowers, and owre the water it cam'. The young men ran doun tae the watter's edge, leapt into the boat, were rowed awa' and up to the second ship. They climbed aboard to a great sound o' welcome, music and laughter. A great company gethered roun' them, haudin' oot cups fu' o' wine. But even as oor young men tasted them, the cups fell. There was a skreich o' dread, a cloud o' darkness, the water swirled aboot the ships and they sank doun, doun into the swirlin' tide. Nae mair was e'er seen or heard o' them. But the ships ha'e come back, and aye they ha'e ta'en a victim.'

'That's a true tale, Mark MacMoran,' said the old wife. 'And there's mair forbye. The end we may na live to see. I mind weel another nicht. It was Hallowe'en, and we'd a' been burnin' nuts and luikin' into the future. I cam' doun here, my lane, weariet and sad at he'rt. Little use for me to luik into the future, the past held a' that I cared for; my gude man and oor braw sons had been drouned here. I sat doun here on a rock. The tide was comin' in fast; the mune was bricht. I saw owre there, staunin' in the water, howkin' at the bank, a man in grey claes, his face grey and his hair. I thocht it maun be the ghaist o' auld Adam Gowdgowpen the miser, condemned, they said, to dig for gowd for ever. Then I saw him dig oot what luiked like a shoe made o' brass. He flung it into the tide; it birled roun' and turned into a boat; he loupit in an' sailed awa' owre to the haunted ships that lay there. Syne the wrecks became two bonny ships in full sail, an' his ain joined them an' the three sailed awa', wi' track o' flame ahint them. But noo I maun back to my ain fireside, for it grows late and I'm weariet. It'll no' be lang ere my auld banes lie in the cauld kirkyaird.'

She tottered away. The young men noticed that she was well happed up against the cold, in a good cloak, and that her feet were well shod. Old Mark was looking after her with the glimmer of a smile on his face, which had previously been so sad and stern.

'Aye, gang yer wa's, Moll Murray. I doubt na' ye'll set yer table wi' gude white breid and wine and cheese, an' sit by a warm hearth. She's gey bien, and nane can say whence that comes, for her man was a puir fisherman. There was a time whan she wad ha'e been named an' tried as a witch. I ken mair than one douce, wyse wumman that has a spray o' rowans abune her door or wears the bonny red berries for fear Moll casts the eye on them, and a farmer that aye drives his cattle wi' a branch o' rowan to guard them frae her glance. Aweel, let that pass.'

He was silent again for a time. Then one of the young men said: 'Have you no more tales on the haunted ships?'

Mark looked at them kindly. 'Aye, I'll tell ye ane that isna canny, but it ends weel. It is no aboot the de'il or aboot ghaists. It's aboot yon Ither People, the elves, the Gude People as some ca' them.

'There was a douce man, Sandie MacHarg, a laird wi' some gude land and gude sheep and cattle. Ae nicht he want oot in his boat wi' his salmon net, and he rowed near the haunted ships. They were baith lit up and there were voices and laughter, and he heard the sound of an axe. Then one voice speired: "What's that ye're makin?" And anither answered: "It's a wife for Sandie MacHarg," and baith voices laughed, a laugh no sae gude tae hear.

'Sandie drew in his net, rowed ashore and went home as fast as he could. He locked and barred the doors and forbade ony in his hoose to open, nae matter wha micht come. Then he bade wife and bairns and servants gether for family prayers. He read a chapter in the Bible; he said a prayer. His wife was surprised, but she speired nae questions. They a' ga'ed to their beds.

'At midnight there was the sound o' hooves. A rider cam' up to the door, knocked loudly and cried oot: "Mistress, ye're wantit, sair wantit, at Laird Laurie's. His wife is brocht to bed, the bairn will be born ony minute, and there's nane to help her but yersel."

'"Sandie's kind wife was awake, beginnin' to dress, ready to gang and help, but Sandie said: "Bide whaur ye are, and dinna answer. Let nane open the door."

'"But, Sandie, the puir wumman is in sair need. There's been nae sign o' a bairn till noo, an' they've been merriet fifteen years and mair."

'"I carena if they've been merriet two score or mair, or if a' the wives in the countryside are cryin' for ye. Ye're no' gaun oot the nicht."

' "What ails ye, Sandie, at Laird Laurie an' his wife? This is no' like ye."

' "Nocht ails me at them," Sandie tel't her. "It's no frae them this summons cam'. To them that sent it we need send nae apology, nae greetin'."

'E'en as he spak', they heard the clatter o' hooves again, and the rider rushin' awa' wi' cries o' rage and curses.

' "Doun on yer knees, lass, and thank the Lord wha has keepit you safe from yon folk. Had ye ridden awa' ye'd ne're ha'e come back, or at least no' for a hunner years and mair."

'And Sandie MacHarg gave thanks to God and prayed to be defended against bogles and ghaists, elves and fiends an' a' the pooers o' darkness, the spirits that wander the earth to tempt mankind.

'His prayer was barely ended whan there was a blaze o' licht ootbye. They saw stable and barn and byre in a muckle fire, the like o't nane had seen. They heard the stamping and neighing of horses, the bellowing of cows. The men servants rushed in: "Laird, we maun save the puir beasts. Unbar the door and lat us oot."

' "Bide whaur ye are. Nane gaes oot frae the hoose this nicht. That fire was no' lit by mortan hauns. Bide and see."

' "Gude defend us," muttered the servants.

' "He will that," Sandie tauld them.

'An' afore lang the flames died down, the horses and cattle were quaiet, stable and byre and barn still stood. The Laird gi'ed thanks to God. At last the household could sleep.

'In the morning when a halesome licht filled the sky, the Laird opened the door into the yard. A' was in order, except that by the door he found a rough-carved wooden figure o' a wumman.

' "Sae that's the wife they ha'e made for me," he said, with a grim chuckle. "Aye, my dear, that was to tak your place whan you were carried awa' to their ain place – had I opened the door to them."

'His wife luiked and trembled, an thocht mair than ever o' her man's wisdom. He took the uncanny thing to the minister and tauld him the hale story. The minister commended him and counselled him to burn the figure. This was dune, an' there was an unco reek frae the flames. But the figure left only a haunfu' o' black ash. Beside this lay – an' here's an unco thing – a braw cup of gowd, elfin wark, fairy treasure. The minister and elders debated the matter, and gi'ed judgment; Sandie had won. The Ither People bore no malice. Lat him keep the bonny cup. An' he and his wife drank frae it till the end o' their lives thegither.'

Old Mark ended his tale and smiled gently to the two young men. They thanked him, said goodbye to him and his bonny granddaughter, pushed their boat into the quiet water and rowed away from the Bay of the Haunted Ships.

Source:
Allan Cunningham, *Traditional Tales of the English and Scottish Peasantry*

Cousin Mattie

The farmer of Finagle and his wife were a decent and a happy couple. They had two children, Flora – a bonny girl of twelve – and Sandy, who was six. Two other children (a girl and a boy) had been born between those two and had died very young. Then a third child had joined them, Matilda, or Mattie, an orphan niece, gladly and lovingly adopted. She was seven years old, and she and Sandy were constant playmates, a lively pair who had many a ploy. Flora – the older in years – was a little apart, though very gentle and kind-hearted, a quiet child very like her mother, who had more than a touch of the dreamer about her.

Early one morning the three children were lying awake in bed, Flora by herself, and Mattie and Sandy sharing a bed. Flora was listening to the younger ones chattering away:

'Do you ever dream, Sandy?' asked Mattie.

'What is it like, to dream?' Sandy asked in turn.

'It's to think you do something you dinna really do.'

'Och, I ken fine aboot that. I'm aften awa' in the green wood wi' Robin Hood and his men. We hunt the deer and ha'e a graun' time,' declared Sandy. 'An' I've seen Thamas the Rhymer ride by wi' the Fairy Queen.'

'But were ye asleep when you saw him?'

'Och na; I was awake. I was jist pretendin' but I likit it a'.'

'Aweel, dreams are different,' Mattie told him. 'They come to ye and whiles they are fearsome. Yestreen I dreamed a bonny leddy cam' to me wi' a red rose and a white rose. She bade me choose the ane I likit, and I chose the white, for och it was bonny, white as snaw and bricht as a star, and it smelt sae sweet. The leddy gi'ed it to me and bade me keep it aye. Mony wad ask for it, but if I gi'ed it awa', I wad dee.'

'An' what happened next?' demanded Sandy. Flora listened without saying a word.

'The leddy tauld me that you yersel' wad ask for the rose, and ye did, Sandy. I had it in my briest, and ye wantit it, and when I wadna gie it to ye, ye grat sair and said I didna love ye. Then I gi'ed ye the rose, and the bonny leddy cam' back luiking sorrowfu', and tel't me I wad dee and that it wad be you yersel', Sandy, that wad kill me, fourteen days from now. Syne I woke and I was greetin', and och, Sandy, I was sair feart.'

'That leddy was tellin' a big lee,' declared Sandy. 'Ye ken fine I wad ne'er kill ye, Mattie. I lo'e ye owre weel. I wadna kill onyone, 'cept mebbe ane o' Robin Hood's men gin we fell oot.'

He chuckled at the thought, and Mattie laughed too, and then the pair of them fell asleep again.

Flora lay thinking, for she had listened with fear and sadness. Her mother, she knew, believed in dreams and had told her of many that had come true, that had been portents and warnings. This was an ill dream. She was sure that Sandy would never deliberately kill Mattie, but he was a strong and lively boy, and he could be impetuous in play, not knowing his own strength. It could happen that he might run at Mattie, knock her over, knock her into the river or even strike her without meaning to hurt.

But it was time to rise, for the sounds of the farm filled the air already. Her mother came in from the milking to rouse the children. Flora said nothing about that dream of Mattie's; it would have distressed her mother, and Mattie herself appeared to have forgotten it. But she thought and thought, and she made a plan.

'Mither,' she said, later that day. 'It's lang since I saw Auntie Jean. Will ye no lat me gang to her for a week or sae. She's aye said I'd be welcome. An' let me tak' Mattie wi' me.'

Her mother listened, smiled and shook her head. 'But what wad I dae wantin' ye baith? Ye're a help to me in kitchen and dairy, my lass. I winna say na to yer gaun yersel',' but no' the baith o' ye.'

'But it wad be lanesome on the road by mysel', an' lanesome at nicht in yon big attic. If ye need Mattie at hame, wad ye no lat Sandy come too?'

'Weel, mebbe,' replied her mother. 'We maun spier at yer faither, my lamb.'

Father had nothing against it, and next day Flora and Sandy went off. It was a long walk, and Sandy grew tired.

'I canna ga'e ony further,' he declared, and he sat down by the roadside. 'I'll awa' back hame, and ye can gang on by yersel', Flora.'

Flora was dismayed. Then she pulled a wooden post from the fence. 'Here, Sandy, here's a fine wee horse ye can ride.'

Sandy laughed. He took the stake, mounted it as if it were indeed a wee horse and went off at a fine pace. Flora followed, and before long they came to Auntie Jean's, to a kind welcome, a good supper and deep sleep; and there they stayed happily until the fifteenth day – for Flora kept very careful count after Mattie had told her dream! They came home to find her lively and well, and life at the farm went on peacefully and happily for seven years.

Flora grew to be a bonny young woman, while Mattie and Sandy were no longer just wee bairns.

Flora did not tell her mother about Mattie's dream and her own fear, but she did once talk to her about dreams in general. Were they true portents or were they just mere illusions? But her mother believed firmly that they were sent as warnings. God sent nothing in vain.

Yet there was no warning of the sorrow that came when their dear mother fell sick and died. Flora had to take charge now of house and dairy, and this she did very capably, while Mattie helped her and learned good housewifery. Sandy was working with his father, a good worker, a lively, high-spirited lad.

Mattie was growing into a real beauty. She was like Flora in courtesy and gentleness to everyone, and she was for the most part a blythe lass, but she had moods of sadness and silence.

'What is it, Mattie?' Flora asked her one day when she had been downcast for longer than usual.

'I've had an eerie dream,' Mattie told her.

'Tell me about it.'

'I wish I needna, but it will comfort me to tell it. Yestreen I dreamed that our dear mother cam' to me, sad and sorrowful. She cam' weeping and she bade me leave here or else great ill wad come. And och, Flora, it wad break my he'rt to leave.'

Flora was no less troubled, but what could be done? Mattie had no other kindred.

Meanwhile Flora had been collecting admirers, one of whom was her special sweetheart – a young farmer, an excellent fellow whom her father liked and welcomed. It was some time before she could be persuaded to leave her father and Mattie and Sandy, but at last they decided to get married. Though he knew he would miss her about the house, her father wanted to see her happily settled. Mattie was proving a good little housewife. She seemed to be happy, and she had never spoken of that second dream.

So Flora married and went away with her husband. There was not a great deal of coming and going between the two households, for the distance between meant a journey of some hours which neither could spare. Then Flora's babies arrived, and she was very busy and very happy, until one day came a rush and shock of grief, in a letter from her father bidding her husband attend, if he could, the funeral of 'my niece, Matilda' a day or two hence. The letter was brief and formal, giving no detail of the cause or manner or even the date of Mattie's death. Flora was nearly demented by shock and grief. Her good husband feared to leave her, but she begged him to go and to bring back all the news he could about Mattie and about her father and Sandy. Her mind was dark with foreboding.

When her husband returned, he had little to tell. Nothing had been told him of the cause of death, whether Mattie had been ill or had died suddenly. Sandy had not been there. He could only tell the day of her death. Flora, who had a very clear memory, realized that it was exactly fourteen years since that morning when she had listened to Mattie telling Sandy about her dream of the bonny lady who gave her the white rose and bade her keep it safely, and of her giving it to Sandy when he demanded it. She was almost frantic with terror.

'Tak' me there,' she implored. 'Tak' me to Mattie's grave. There is mair here than has been tauld. I maun ken. Och but we should ha'e paid heed to my mither's warning!'

Her husband did his best to comfort her, but only one thing would help. He must take her to the kirkyard where Mattie lay, buried in the same grave as her mother. So on the Sunday he took her behind him on his horse, and they rode off to her old home: not to the farm, only to the kirkyard, and there he set her down as she desired, to go by herself to the grave with its new piles of turf.

She wrapped her cloak about her, drawing the hood about her face, and walked quietly to the grave. It was by a low wall where an old woman and an old man sat talking. She knew them both, but their backs were towards her, and they neither saw her nor heard her approach.

'Saw ye the puir lassie in her coffin?' asked the man. 'They tell me that nane did, that there was nae kistin'.'

'Deed there wasna, but I was there. Och but she was a bonny lass and a gentle, aye wi' a kindly word for a', and she was like a dochter to her uncle. He is sair stricken, puir man. I'll tell ye, for I ken ye're a discreet man that winna speak, what I've tel't nane ither. Puir Mattie wasna' lyin' her lane in her coffin. There she was in her windin' sheet, her face bonnier than ever, and there on her briest lay a new-born babe that hadna lived but for an hour; a wee white rose barely in bud.'

Source:
James Hogg, *The Ettrick Shepherd's Tales*

George Dobson Drives to Hell

The roads to hell are many and the journey there can be swift. None would have looked to find George Dobson upon it, for he was known as a decent, well-doing man, owner of a hackney coach and horses, dependable for a hire and a journey. But you never know.

He thought he knew the country round Edinburgh where he lived, and all the villages, but when a gentleman whom he had served more than once came and asked to be taken to one place, George did not know the name at all.

'I'll drive ye there if ye'll direct me.'

'But surely you know the way? It is no great distance.'

'I'll drive ye to hell if ye'll direct me.'

'So! Then take us up, my son here and myself, and drive on. You need have no fear of the road.'

His passengers mounted, George drove off, and never had his horses taken the road so swiftly. They went spanking on in great style. The road seemed always to lead downhill. There was no pause, there were no toll-gates. At last George decided he must stop for the sake of the horses, and not before time. They were panting and sweating now. He climbed down and opened the coach door.

The day had passed from light to dusk and now to darkness. He was about to tell his passengers that he could drive no further until the horses were rested, but the gentleman descended, followed by his son, and assured George that they had reached their journey's end. 'So you may go now, but you must return for us tomorrow at the hour of noon precisely.'

'And whit aboot my payment?' There was a debt owing from this passenger already.

'That will all be settled tomorrow, and the toll-money as well.'

'There was no toll-gate on the road.'

'There was, but you did not see it. It is not far back from here. You will not be allowed to pass this time without some token. Take this card. It will ensure your passing. I have no money on me.'

'Ye never have,' said George grimly. 'Ye owe me for mair nor ane ride.'

'It will all be settled, I tell you, tomorrow. Now take the card.'

George took it. There were words on it, written in red ink, but George could not read.

'Whaur is the toll-gate? Whit wey did they no' ask us to pay as we cam' by?'

'There is no road out of here but the one we came by. So none can escape the toll, whether coming or going. Did you not see a group of men in dark clothes standing by a gate?'

'Och aye. But yon was no toll. It was the gate into the grounds o' a great hoose. I ken some of the men we saw. I've driven them in the toun an' they've never been short o' money. Gude fellows, gentlemen o' the law.'

'Well, be here tomorrow at noon precisely.'

The gentleman and his son disappeared into the thick blackness of night. George mounted the box again. He could hardly see his horses, hardly hear the sound of their hooves as they moved, if they were moving at all. There was a great rushing of wind, as of flame, which confused his hearing as the darkness did his sight. Yet they must have moved, for he saw the gate he had passed on the way, and two men standing there whom he knew, two young lawyers whom he had often driven to their suppers and their frolics. He greeted them cheerfully, remembering their friendly talk and jesting. But they stood utterly silent, pointing to the gate. There stood the toll-keeper, and a grim, black carle he was, of immense height and breadth of shoulder. The gate was closed.

'Why are these young gentlemen standing here?' asked George.

'Because they are the last comers. This nicht they maun mind the gate wi' me. The morn's morn ye shall take owre frae them.'

'The devil I wull!'

'Aye, the devil ye wull.'

'I'll be damned if I do.'

'Aye, ye'll be damned.'

'Let me go, ye ruffian. Open the gate. Let go my horses' – for the gate-keeper was holding the reins.

'Aye, I'll open the gate and let the horses go.'

The man swung the gate open, came up to the coach, dropped the reins and caught George in his great arms, swinging him down from the box. The horses rushed madly off. George struggled and cursed, neither of which had any effect. His adversary held him firm.

'Help me. Can ye no' help me?' George appealed to the two young lawyers, strong young fellows. 'Ye ken me weel. I've driven ye mony a time oot to the country, you and the bonny leddies ye said were yer sisters – but I doubted that. I took them and you, when nae ither coachman would, on the Sabbath.'

But the young men, once so friendly, were silent, pointing to the gate.

George spoke again to the gate-keeper. 'Let me gang. Wha are ye? By what richt dae ye haud me?'

'By what richt? D'ye no ken whaur ye are?'

'I do not, and I demand to be told.'

'Aweel, it's my pleisure to tell ye. Ye're in hell. An' here ye'll bide to open the gate to wha'e'er comes next.' He looked at George with a fiendish grin.

George remembered the card given him by the gentleman. He took it from his pocket and showed it.

'Och aye; ye had this frae yon gentleman wha, wi' his son, has been lang expected here. He bids me let ye gang noo. But ye maun be back here the morn, at twal' o' the clock. He's put his name to it, and ye maun dae the same.'

'I'll dae nae sic thing.'

'Then ye'll bide here.' The gate-keeper swung the gate shut.

Poor George fell on his face, weeping. He thought of his good wife. If only he could see her again. She might help him . . .

A voice spoke. It was his wife's, and her hand touched him. 'Geordie, Geordie, wauken and get up. D'ye no' ken the time? Ye should ha'e been up an hour ago. Ye're to tak' the Lord President to Parliament House. Get up, I'm tellin' ye.'

George struggled up, bewildered. There stood Kirsty, his wife, half laughing, half scolding.

'Wumman, hoo can I drive the Lord President to Parliament Hoose when my puir horses are lamed if they're no' deid?'

Kirsty laughed. 'Man, Geordie, ye're still dreamin'. Ye shouldna ha'e ta'en that extra dram last nicht. I tel't ye. The coach is ready, the horses are harnessed. Yer man Jock has seen to that. It's only yersel' that's no ready. Get up, or I'll throw a pail o' watter owre ye.'

'But I canna gang to Parliament Hoose e'en wi' the Lord President. I maun be yonder at twal' noon.'

'Whaur's yonder? Ye'll be back frae Parliament Hoose lang ere noon.'

But Kirsty was beginning to feel alarmed. She went out to the stable to bid Jock tidy himself and take the coach to the Lord President's house. When she returned, George was still lying, groaning. He was like a man paralysed.

In deep distress she went to Dr Sandy Wood, a wise and good physician whose wisdom held more than medical knowledge, and plenty of that too.

He listened to Kirsty with grave attention and spoke kindly. 'So he says he maun keep the tryst at twal' o' the clock. Faith, he maunna dae that. Put the clock back an hour or mair, keep him as quiet as ye can an' I'll come an' see him as soon as I can. Ha'e ye ocht mair to tell me?'

Kirsty told him everything she had heard from her husband, who had been babbling and raving as she thought; she told him about the gentleman and the toll-keeper and the two young lawyers.

Dr Wood looked very grave. 'I'd better come wi' ye noo.'

They walked off together, Kirsty hardly able to keep up with the doctor's long strides.

'The puir young fellows,' he said, speaking of the two lawyers. 'They're baith deid. They died yestreen at the same hour, o' the same malignant fever. Did George say the name o' the gentleman wha engaged him?'

'Aye, I think I mind o' it' – and Kirsty spoke the name of a gentleman well known, of good family and position.

'But he's in London, he and his son.'

They came to the house and found George still lying inert, his face turned to the wall.

Dr Wood felt his pulse and looked closely at him.

'He has a fever. Bring vinegar to wash his head and face and hands.' The doctor himself made a poultice for the patient's head and his feet.

'I maun get up. I maun drive to the tryst at twal' noon,' George cried, suddenly starting up.

'Deed, but ye maun lie still,' commanded the doctor.

Kirsty went out again to fetch their minister, a good man and wise. He, she felt sure, would banish the evil spirit which possessed her husband. But before he came, the clock struck twelve, and with no more words George died.

Next day news came of a great storm at sea, in which a ship sailing from London had sunk with all on board. Among them were that gentleman and his son who had engaged George to drive them and had bidden him keep the tryst at twelve noon.

Source:
James Hogg, *The Ettrick Shepherd's Tales*

Adamson of Laverhope
and the Devil

A tempestuous man may be destroyed by tempest, or one possessed by cruelty and rage may be taken by the master of all evil, who may sometimes control the forces of nature as a man uses a weapon. Demoniac rage in a man may be confronted and overwhelmed by demoniac power.

Adamson, farmer of Laverhope, was a man of substance and good standing, respected by some for his wealth, by many for his upright and godly way of life, regular in attendance at kirk, known to be earnest in prayer and in searching the Scriptures. But by some he was less liked. He was a hard man and of fierce temper, easily roused. For any debt, for any mischief done, he demanded full payment.

So it went ill with another farmer, a neighbour, one Irvine, who was far from prosperous, a feckless poor fellow with whom nothing went well. Adamson lent him money with a show of benevolence that made Irvine believe he would be an easy creditor. But when he could not pay, he found Adamson inexorable. There was more fuel for the rich man's anger. A herd laddie on Irvine's farm had, in sheer silly mischief, been chasing some of Adamson's cattle, doing them no real harm. A clout on his lug would have been punishment enough but Adamson was enraged, and when Irvine came to him saying that he could not pay, begging for time, he was like the malignant servant in the Gospel parable who, although he himself had been forgiven a large debt, would not listen to his fellow-servant who owed him so little but had him thrown into prison. And so Adamson dealt with poor feckless Irvine.

Not only was he to be kept in prison till he should pay his debt, but his cattle and all his gear were to be sold and his wife and the children turned out of their house. It would take all that to repay Adamson.

If Irvine, however, was a weak character who submitted to his sentence, his wife was far different: a strong, outspoken woman; some called her a randy, but she was fearless and loyal.

'Ye canna dae this to my puir bairns, ane but a babe, an' to me forbye what ye ha'e dune to my puir man. Ye are drivin' us oot on the road to beg oor bread. If yer bowels o' compassion are no' scorched by the fires o' hell, think on't, tak' pity on us, and maybe there will be pity for yersel' at the hinner end.'

'I have no need of pity. I owe no man any debt. I demand only what is due to me. Yer man maun pey me the sillar he had frae me.'

'Ha'e it ye shall, ilk bawbee. Gi'e me but time to work for it, and ye'll lack nane o'r, neither plack nor bawbee. I gi'e ye my word.'

'Why should I tak' yer word? Yer man didna keep his.'

'Are ye no' feart ye'll be burnt in hell among the merciless?'

'Fient a fear ha'e I. A' I ask is my due. That I maun ha'e.'

'Then I wadna be in your place for a' the gowd an' gear ye ha'e, though I've nane mysel' an' maun tak' to the road wi' my puir bairns, to beg oor bread as weel as I can. We may sleep in barn or byre, we may gang cauld and weet, or there may be kind folk to help us, and may the Lord reward them that do. For such there will be reward hereafter, but for you, Maister Adamson, dule and woe hereafter. Life may be lang or short, blythe or waesome, we can thole it. But eternity is lang, lang, and it may haud dule wi' oot end. Think o' that, Maister Adamson. They that show mercy dae the wark o' the Lord; they that are pitiless serve the de'il, and he is a maister wha demands lang service and tak's his servants in the end. Think weel on that, Maister Adamson.'

'Haud yer haverin' rantin' tongue, woman. What has the De'il to do wi' my affairs, my just demands? Awa' wi' ye, oot o' here.'

The bairns were crying. Their mother said no more but led them away, herself a tall, dark, menacing figure.

The roup (sale) at Irvine's farm took place, and Adamson attended. He put in a bid for Mrs Irvine's favourite cow, and he had it.

'Eh, Bell, my bonny lass,' she lamented. 'The best in the byre. Ye're to gang to that cruel de'il o' a maister. Gude peety us a' noo, but peety him maist at the hinner en' an' gar him repent.'

There were, as she had hoped, kind neighbours to help her with food and clothes, with a night's shelter, with work that would earn some bawbees. There was much condemnation of Adamson, but not by everyone. There were those who declared he had taken only his due; he was an upright man, going regularly to the kirk, known to be a man of prayer; and he was a man of means and of substance.

The sheep-shearing began and, as was usual, Adamson went up to the hill with his own shepherds, some from other farms and some of his crofters. He carried the branding iron with which the sheep would be marked as his. He was in a foul temper, part resentment at Mrs Irvine, part a sense of guilt he would not admit to himself, and his mood was exacerbated by the talk and laughter of the herds. It hardly needed a touch to set him up in a blaze, and the touch came in the barking and laring of a young dog, Nimble, which belonged to one of his own herd-laddies. Adamson struck the poor beastie with the branding iron. It fell, howling piteously. Men looked up in horror. Even the roughest of them was kindly towards the dogs.

The boy came running from the gate of the fold where he was holding in the sheep that were to be shorn. He left the gate open, and they all bundled out.

'Nimble, my puir Nimble,' he cried, running to his beloved companion. 'What ails ye, Nimble? Och, ye're hurtit to deith. What'll I dae wantin' ye?'

The dog was lying still. The men looked on silently, pityingly. Adamson lost control, what control he had ever had. He seized the boy by the hair, dragged him away and began thrashing him. Then one of the shepherds, Rob Johnston, a man of great height and strength, rose and came forward. He caught Adamson by the arms in a grip of iron, holding him fast until he dropped his hold on the boy. Adamson was in a maniac rage now. He struggled furiously but was helpless in that strong hold. The boy ran back, sobbing, to his dear Nimble.

Rob Johnston spoke: 'What ails ye, Maister Adamson? Are ye clean mad? Is the De'il himsel' in ye that ye are like to kill the laddie as ye've killed his doug?'

He towered over Adamson as the latter had over the laddie. He held him fast – and he held his own rage.

'Let me go. Daur ye speak to me like that?'

'I'll haud ye fast, an' I daur speak, and ye'll staun' to hear me. If ye dinna, ye'll ga'e doun on yer back. I'll throw you and staun' owre ye. Think, man, on what ye ha'e dune to this puir orphan laddie wha has nane to love him but his doug. They ha'e served ye well, baith laddie an' doug. The De'il is in ye the day. See that he does not destroy you; see that ye dinna come into the judgement that sends lost souls to hell.'

There was utter silence. Some of the lassies there had been screaming, some crying; the men had been growling in honest wrath. But now even the sobs of the poor herd-laddie were stilled. Rob loosed his grasp. Adamson went sullenly away, none speaking to him. The shearers began their work again, none speaking, but there was menace in the air.

Then an old gaberlunzie man appeared from over the hill: Patie Maxwell, a well-known character. He walked leaning on his stick, carrying his poke. It was likely he would be given some shorn wool. Folk were good to him, giving him meal and bread and cheese, letting him sleep in the barn. He was genial, with plenty of news to tell. The bairns liked him, and he was gentle with them. The dogs knew him with a wag of the tail and never a growl.

He spoke first to Adamson, who had drawn away, sullenly, from the others. 'Hoo's a' wi' ye the day, Maister Adamson? Ye ha'e a fine flock here, an' it's a graun day for the shearin'.'

'I'm nane the better o' you. Awa' oot o' here afore I gar ye, and see ye comena back.'

'Hoots, mon, that's no wey to talk. I'll gang when I like an' whaur I like.'

'Ye'll gang noo. I'll no' ha'e ye keepin' my men frae their wark wi' yer havers.'

'Me keep them frae their wark? They a' ken me. I'll just bide an' rest my auld banes.'

'Ye'll no' bide here, ye auld Papist doug.'

'Wha are ye ca'in a Papist doug?'

'Yersel' an' nane ither. It's weel kent ye're ane o' them that kiss a cross an' boo doun to a crozier and rattle beads an' mumble prayers. It's a shame that the likes o' you should be at large to pester gude Protestants. If ye dinna gang oot o' here, I'll ha'e ye afore the magistrates.'

'Aye, I'm Catholic, sure enough. I've aye held to the auld religion, an' nane o' the gude folk here ha'e questioned my richt to pray as I please.'

'Haud yer tongue and ga'e oot o' here, auld wafer-eater and worshipper o' graven images, or I'll . . .'

'Ye'll what? I'm thinkin' I'll bide.'

Adamson again lost control – the little he had. He ran at the old gaberlunzie with mad force, knocking him down. Patie's poke fell, scattering the meal and bits of bread folk had given him and some bits of fleece. His cloak fell off, into the burn.

Patie picked himself up, unbroken, but the shaking had roused his temper. He seemed to tower over Adamson as Rob Johnston had towered, and he spoke with a voice none had heard from him before, with authority: 'I ha'e drawn sword and spear fechtin' for the richtfu' King, him owre the watter, fechtin' against mony a better man than you, Maister Adamson. In the Name o' the Holy Trinity and oor Blessed Lady and a' the saints, I bid ye tak' tent.'

'We's better gang to the help o' the auld gaberlunzie,' one of the shepherds said to Rob Johnston.

'I'm thinkin' it's Adamson that'll need help,' said Rob. 'The auld gaberlunzie has focht wi' better men in his time. I'd rather be wi' him than against him, Papist though he be . . . But ye'd better be gettin' on wi' the shearin'.'

Someone had picked up the beggar's poke; someone else plucked his cloak from the burn.

Patie stood looking at Adamson. 'In the Name o' the Holy Trinity and oor Blessed Lady, I bid you go to your ain place.'

Adamson skulked away, no one paying much attention to him. Patie stood, looking more himself again.

'I ne'er heard ye curse afore,' one old shepherd told him. Ye've aye be weel-spoken an' jokesome and gentle wi' the bairns. Are ye no' feart to invoke the Powers like that?'

'I ha'e invoked them before, the Powers of heaven and of hell. I invoke them now against that man o' sin. His end will be destruction.'

The two protagonists were strangely altered. The man of wealth and power, the master, was sullen and cowed; the auld gaberlunzie clothed with a new dignity, with something awesome about it.

The day was wearing on, the light fading. Suddenly a great cloud appeared in the sky, almost a gathering together of clouds. Rob was to describe it years later as a dark whirlpool that swallowed the light as a flood of darkness.

'Luik there,' cried Patie, 'see that unco cloud. The curse o' God is in it.'

'Haud yer profane tongue,' cried the old shepherd who had spoken before. 'A Papist canna pretend to ken the will o' the Almighty.'

'Ye think weel o' yersel's, you Protestants,' retorted Patie. 'Ye may mock at us Papists, but ye ken nocht ava aboot religion, aboot prayer, aboot the power o' God. Luik there at the cloud. It grows greater and blacker, a cloud o' doom an' death. Doun on yer knees an' see if yer prayers will be heard.'

The cloud was indeed menacing beyond anything any of them had seen.

'We maun fauld the sheep,' ordered Rob. 'There will be sic a tempest as nane o' us has seen.'

The cloud grew until it covered the sky. It burst into torrents of rain. The river flooded over the field, lightning flashed, thunderbolts fell from the mirk sky; the crash was like the sudden dissolution, the perdition, of the earth.

Patie stood laughing, a horrible, devilish laughter, as if

possessed by the Devil, as if he were the Devil himself, mocking, triumphing.

The flood swept away the flocks of the rich man.

'The De'il is in ye. Or are ye the De'il himsel'?' the old shepherd called to Patie.

'Na, na, I'm no the De'il. I'd show ye some ferlies if I were. Is it no a strange thing that an auld gaberlunzie like mysel' should ha'e sic power, when you godly Calvinists ha'e nane ava, ha'e nae knowledge of the powers and mysteries beyond this earth? Aye, it wad be sublime to be the De'il himself. Ye puir chickens o' Calvin pay heed to the auld Coppersmith and the Black Cloud.'

'Whaur's Adamson?' called someone.

'He's gane up to that hut,' another shepherd answered. 'He'll be gane there to pray, nae doot.'

The storm increased in violence and darkness. A great flight of crows was flying overhead with wild croaking and crying, easier to be heard than to be seen in the darkness.

'Yon's a graun flicht o' corbies,' said the gaberlunzie with an evil chuckle. 'Hark to them, makin' their mane.'

Then suddenly the darkness cleared. Through the black cloud came a rift of purest blue, most heavenly, most tranquil colour, and with it a gleam, then a radiance of sun. The rain had ceased. The wild wind was still; the black flight of corbies had dispersed. The earth looked as it might have done after the flood. The old beggar had disappeared.

'It's no' canny,' said one man.

'We'd better find Maister Adamson,' said another.

A herd-laddie began to run towards the hut. They looked after him and saw him stand in the doorway, look in, then turn and come out.

'Let him be,' called the old shepherd. 'He has fell need to be at his prayers. But what ails the lad?'

The lad began running up the hill, in a strange zigzag course, as if following a track, picking up footsteps. Suddenly he stopped, turned and waved his arms. The men began to come up to him and saw his look of stark horror and its cause.

There on the ground lay the body of the rich man. He had been struck by lightning, one side so riven that his bowels had gushed out. Beside him was a newly dug, shallow grave. But who had dug it? There was no trace of anyone else.

That was the most fearful death ever known. And no less fearful was the news that came next day, the certain news that Patie Maxwell, the auld gaberlunzie, had not been near that part. He had been seen by many, had talked to them, had been his canny, genial, even jocose self in a part of the countryside miles away, too far for him to travel in a day. Folk there heard of the flood, of the awful cloud, of the marvellous return of sun and of that radiant, heavenly blue.

Had the Devil truly been – not in the decent auld Patie himself, but in a likeness of him that he had taken by his Satanic power? Yet Patie in that likeness had spoken not only curses but the Name of the Holy Trinity, the name of the Blessed Virgin, which all evil creatures, devils, warlocks and all, abhor.

Only two things were known. Patie Maxwell had not been in or near that region on that day. And Adamson, the man of merciless and evil temper, had died a most horrible death, and his grave had been dug by his side.

Source:
James Hogg, *The Ettrick Shepherd's Tales*

The Sleep-walker of Redcleugh

(The tale is told by a doctor of a sleep-walker, haunted or possessed, of a house shadowed by doom, of a book lost . . .)

I was summoned to the old house of Redcleugh to the widow of the late laird, Mr Bernard: summoned by his kinsman and trustee Mr Gordon. He wrote me that the lady was still young, still in health of body but suffering from alienation of mind. She had been sleep-walking. There was some dark tragedy behind it. The old house was darkened. There was no legend of a family ghost or such uncanniness, only this darkness.

And this I realized when I went there. Mrs Bernard was indeed young, and she was beautiful, fair of complexion with large blue eyes which could look gentle and loving but were full of fear as if some wild demon possessed her and looked out of those eyes. She would not speak.

There was little I could do. I prepared a soothing draught and bade the woman servant (who appeared to be maid, cook, housekeeper all in one) to see her to bed. It was a baffling case. Mr Gordon had told me so little.

I was to stay the night. Presently I was served, by the old butler (his name, he told me, was Andrew), with dinner: a plain meal but well cooked and ample, and with it a Burgundy that would have made a bannock and cheese into a banquet.

I praised it to Andrew, who was pleased. 'Aye, sir, it's guid wine an' auld. The laird keepit a fine cellar like his faither afore him. An' noo there's nane to enjoy it. The heir is but a bairn, wee Caleb.'

He sighed and then, judging me to be a sympathetic listener, began talking about his late master with great affection, and of his father before him. 'It was a fine hoose then.' Of the change that had come, of that poor lady his mistress, widowed and alone, he said nothing.

I was tired; it had been a long journey to Redcleugh, beyond the bounds of my usual calls, so I asked to be taken to my room. He left me there, with a candle lit. Once in bed, though I was warm and comfortable enough, I could not sleep. The great room was full of shadows. I am not fanciful, but it seemed to be filled with sadness, with mystery. After a few restless moments I rose, took the candle and began looking for anything, any book that would pass the time or send me to sleep. I had none with me. But there was not so much as a pamphlet anywhere.

The candle lit up four portraits on the walls, two of children: a boy, handsome, proud, dark, very dark, with more than the darkness found in our northern families; the other of a tiny girl, hardly out of babyhood, as fair and golden as the boy was dark. The boy looked as if he had been touched by too bright a sun; the girl as if touched by too pale a moon. Then there were two portraits of ladies, one of a loveliness and grace beyond anything I had seen, dark of hair and eyes, very gentle, with a sadness about the face that enhanced the gentle beauty. Mr Bernard, I knew, but no more than this, had been twice married. Was the dark lady his first wife, and the mother of the boy? The other portrait I recognized as that of my patient, golden-fair and beautiful, and with a happy and loving look now lost and shadowed.

I walked round the room and looked into a cupboard, into shelves, but found no book. Then I came to an old cabinet and began trying the drawers. They were very stiff, hard to open, especially the one at the top. Something was stuck at the back. I pulled again and again, harder and harder, and the drawer yielded violently, almost knocking me over. There at the back was stuffed a thick bundle of paper – a book, shabby, crumpled, but an undoubted book.

Smoothing it flat, I read by the light of my candle: *The true and genuine history of the murderer Jane Grierson, who poisoned her mistress, and thereby became the wife of her master, James Temple.* The date was 1742. I had not heard of this murder, but I am no expert in the literature of Newgate. On the top of the title-page was written, in a clear, recent hand, the name Amelia Bernard. How had the family of Redcleugh come to be connected with that of Temple – with Jane Grierson? Did the clue lie there to the tragedy that seemed to possess the house, to the wandering mind of its mistress?

I took the book with me back to bed and was about to begin my reading when I heard slow, heavy footsteps in the passage, then a knock at the door, and old Andrew came in. I laid the book aside – I had seen only the title, the inscription 'Amelia Bernard' and a picture of a woman's face, wild, staring.

'Yer pardon if I disturb ye, sir. But it has aye been my duty to go round the hoose ere I go to my bed, and see ilk licht extinguished. That has been dune ever since Miss Marjory, the auld laird's aunt, wha used to read her auld romances late into the nicht, set fire to her bed – and her room – and the hale east wing.'

'I am glad to see you, Andrew,' I told him. 'Tell me – who are these children, and who is the dark, beautiful lady? The fair lady I recognize as my patient – as she must have been in a happier time.'

'Aye, sir, that is my Leddy Amelia, my late master's second wife. The ither is the Leddy Lillah, his first wife, the mither o' the laddie, Maister Caleb. The wee lass is Miss Mary, dochter of the Leddy Amelia.'

So – Amelia Bernard. The mystery darkened.

Andrew continued. 'The Laird was aye a traveller, an' no just owre the watter to France an' Italy like some o' the gentry, but to faur pairts, to the East whaur folks arena Christian but worship Allah and his prophet Mahomet. I've heard him discoorse on that. Weel, he brocht hame a bride, that leddy there, and och she was the loveliest floo'er I ha'e seen: Rose o' Sharon as it says in the Guid Buik. To luik at her was to hear a melody, aye, and her voice was a sang in every word she spak. She had the English, though pairt o' the time she and the Laird spak' in her ain tongue. Christy, my wife, an' I agreed we had never heard sound sae sweet as her voice.'

'You are a poet, Andrew,' I told him.

'The man wha has seen sich beauty – ony kind o' beauty – canna but be a poet, be he scholar or noble or puir and untaught. The laird fair worshipped her, and she loo'ed him wi' her hale he'rt. We spak' o' it, Christy an' mysel'. Christy was feart. They were owre deep in love, owre happy; it couldna last. We're no' meant to be sae happy. An' it didna last: the love did but no' the happiness. Ane day a great lord or prince cam' in a strange equipage wi' his attendants. He cam' frae the East. I wasna tel't but I thocht, an' Christy thocht, it was my leddy's faither come in wrath and vengeance. He was the mair enraged, it was fearsome, when she tauld him she had renounced the faith o' her race, that she gave no more worship to Allah or obedience to his prophet Mahomet, for she held as Lord, now, Our Blessed Saviour and she loved His Holy Mother. He cursed her then, cursed her husband, their house, the children who might be born to them, and all the race of Bernard, and so departed, terrible in wrath.'

I listened, almost spellbound. The old butler had taken on all the dignity of one of the bards of ancient times.

He was silent for a moment.

'There was a shadow frae that day aboot this auld hoose. Yet it was a fine hoose, wi' servants to care for it and wait on the Laird and his leddy. The Laird likit a guid table, and he had his cellar stocked wi' fine wine, like that ye drank at denner, sir. An' I'm thinkin' ye'd be nane the waur o' another draught o' that.'

His face relaxed a little from its dolour. I thanked him and said again how noble a wine it was. Andrew left the room and came back presently with a goodly goblet of the 'blude-red wine' as the old ballad calls it. I drank a little, gratefully, lay back and listened as Andrew continued.

'For a while there was joy and peace. But aye the darkness lay ahint the licht. The servants felt it; they left, ane by ane, an' the Laird saw few folk; few guests cam' to the hoose. He and his leddy wantit only each ither. Forbye, she was near her time, and it was a sair time for her. Christy was wi' her in her labour, which was lang and sair. She brocht forth a son – there he is, Caleb – as bonny a babe as ony could desire. They were fair wrapped up in him, but my leddy didna gain her strength. She dwined. Christy did a' she could but she couldna be a companion – the puir leddy wantit mother or sister or friend.

'Weel, the nearest gentry were the family at Abbeyfield. There were two dochters, young lassies, wha had a governess, Miss Amelia Temple. They cam' aboot the hoose; the lassies played wi' the bairn. They were growing up; they nae langer needit a governess – an' my leddy, wha likit her weel, pled wi' the Laird to have her come here as companion. He had no likin' for that, at first, but my leddy pled sae, and he could see how fond they were, the two bonny leddies, o' each ither, an' hoo gentle Miss Amelia was wi' the Leddy Lillah and wi' her bairn. So he consentit, and a' seemed to go well – for a time.

'But then my leddy began to dwine, as if the strength were drained frae her. Mebbe ye could have said, Doctor, what ailed her, but I doot if the wisest physician could. An then, ae nicht she left us, quaiet as a shadow, an' a shadow she had become o' her lovely self. There was nae agony. She spak' to the maister wi' deep love; she spak' her faith in Our Lord and Saviour and His Blessed Mother, and she went hame to bliss, I ken, but for her husband and the auld hoose it was desolation.'

Again Andrew paused.

'And then?' I asked.

'Afore she died, my leddy – Christy heard her – said to the maister that he maun wed Amelia for she loo'ed him, and she wad mak' a guid wife an' a kind mither to the bairn. He had declared he could never love a woman as he had loved Leddy Lillah – but in time he cam' to luik mair and mair fondly upon Miss Amelia. She was sae gentle, sae guid to his son. An' sae they were marrit, and the auld hoose lost some o' the mirk, though no' all. In due time oor new mistress was brocht to bed, and the wee lass Mary was born. There was happiness again – though no' for me, for my dear Christy began to dwine awa', and afore that year was oot she was deid. She had likit the new Mrs Bernard and found her kind, but I'm thinkin' something went oot of Christy when the dear Leddy Lillah died. There was peace for a time, though it was a quaiet hoose. Mrs

Bernard was guid to baith bairns, but she didna play wi' them or sing to them as the Leddy Lillah had dune.

'But waur was to come and muckle dule. Ae mornin' I was coming alang the passage here, to the maister's dressing-room – which is through that door – to attend him as was my wont, when the mistress cam' oot, rinnin' like a mad cratur. She didna see me for her handkerchief was at her een and she was sabbin' like ane dementit. She rushed past me and doun the stairs. I ga'ed on into the room but the maister wasna there. I ga'ed into the bedroom, this room ye're in. He was sittin' up in yon chair, in his dressing-gown wi' a stricken look on his face, waur even than he had when the Leddy Lillah died.

'"Maister, maister, whit ails ye?" I speired, and he said: "Andrew, this house is doomed. The curse has fallen upon it."

'"Maister, maister, ye're ill, ye're no' yersel'," I cried an' turned to the door. "Where are you going, Andrew?" he called. I tel't him: "To fetch the mistress."

'"Never again will you do that. Fetch that murderer, that woman who poisoned my Lillah, my beloved who trusted her, that she-devil!"

'"Maister, maister," I cried.' (Andrew seemed to re-enact the scene as if possessed by memory, as if still facing his master and hearing that terrible charge.) He continued more quietly:

'My maister tauld me then that the Leddy Amelia had been restless and had disturbed him. He saw her rise and walk about the room, in her sleep, talking to herself – aye, like Lady Macbeth, no' like her ain sel'. The laird mindit her words an' spak' them: "She stood between me and my love who was her husband – whom I desired for mine, whom I would take. A Grierson ne'er let onyone staun' between him and his desire and I am a Grierson an' I will ha'e my love."

'The maister had asked her then – for she could hear and answer – and she had said that she had given poison, the sleepy poison, to her rival, given it more and more, day by day, until the last sleep fell.

'"An' nane kent what had killed her. They a' thocht she had but pined and dwined awa'. Her husband, my love, was sair stricken, syne he turned to me for comfort – an' I won him. I hold him, he is mine – an' he kens nocht, puir fule."

'Syne the maister tel't me she fell silent, and she cam' back into bed, cauld as a corpse, and lay still. There was nae sleep for him. Bye an' bye she had waukened and turned to kiss him like her ain sel' as she had been. He had shuddered and thrust her from him, called her murderer, cursed her. And she had risen and rin oot – as I had seen her, near dementit.'

'Andrew, you tell me a terrible tragedy. No wonder the poor woman is mad. But – was she guilty?'

'Hear the rest o' my tale, doctor. I left the room then and cam' doun the stairs. My mistress cam' oot frae the library, quaiet noo, but wi' sic a luik, he'rt-broken as I pray ne'er again to see on ony face. She brocht me into the room an' asked me what her husband had told me. I was sweirt to answer, it was sae fearsome, but she bade me tell, for she maun ken. Sae I went owre it a'. And she said: "It is e'en as I feared, Andrew. I ha'e been in a dream, sleep-walking like ane possessed. It is that book. Would that I had ne'er seen it."

'Syne she tel't me. The buik was the story and confession of Jane Grierson, her grandmother, second wife of her grandfather James Temple, whose first wife she had poisoned, from jealousy, from desire to have James Temple for herself. She had not lived, mercifully, to be condemned and hanged; she had died after confessing her crime, whether in remorse or triumph who could say, and soon afterwards the wretched husband had died too. The Leddy Amelia's faither had been a daicent man. The story had not been told his dochter, but she had found this auld book and read it, and brocht it wi' her in her trunk to Redcleugh.

'"Whaur is the buik?" I speired at her, and she tauld me it was in a drawer o' the desk in the dressing-room.

'"Gang noo and find it, Andrew, and show it to my husband. It will be proof of my delusion, my haunting dream – and my innocence."

'Sae back I ga'ed to the Laird and tauld him a'. He listened, he was calm too, he wantit to believe her innocence. He bade me find the buik and bring it to him and he would believe. I went to the desk; I luiked in every drawer; my leddy cam' and luiked wi' me – but no' a page, no' a scrap o' paper could we find. The puir leddy wept. She took me up to the attic where her trunks were stored and luiked in every ane – but no' a token o' the buik was there.

'The Laird went back to his black mood. He wadna speak to her, he wadna see her. He sent for Mr Gordon, him wha sent you here, Doctor. They were closeted lang thegither. The Laird made him his trustee; he sent the bairns back wi' him wi'oot lettin' their mither an' stepmither see them; he arranged wi' Mr Gordon that she wad bide here, her lane, but askit me and the cook, a daicent body, to hide and care for the hoose. Syne he went aff himsel', back to thae faur eastern lands whence he had brocht the lovely Leddy Lillah. An' efter a time there cam' word that he was deid. An' noo, Doctor, ye ken the tale o' Redcleugh, the doom o' the auld hoose.'

'I kent mair than that, Andrew,' I told him, and showed him the book, with the staring, awful face of Jane Grierson.

'Your mistress spoke the truth. It was a dream, an ill dream, a cruel inheritance from that woman, her grandmother. But she herself, I am convinced, is innocent. But she was unbalanced – by the shock of Lillah's death, by the way of that death – a decline, a dwindling like that which the poor first wife of James Temple had suffered through poison. Indeed it would have been well had she never seen that book; if it had been found to prove her delusion, her innocence, but now – what use is it? She is too far gone in her mind. The shock would drive her utterly demented. If indeed she understood anything, it might kill her.'

I told him how and where I had found it.

'Gude kens hoo it got there.'

The poor girl had, I thought, perhaps thrust it away, been confused, thought only of one drawer, then of her trunk. And now – the doom had indeed fallen upon Redcleugh. Pray God, I said, that the children would escape, that they might never know.

Well, I saw my poor patient again, witless as before. I left some soothing medicine, all I could do, bade Andrew and the cook to watch carefully over their mistress and promised to return in a few days. Then I went home.

While I was still considering what to tell Mr Gordon, a letter came from him with startling news. He had heard from his kinsman himself, Mr Bernard, from Aleppo. The Laird of Redcleugh had indeed gone back to the East, where he had wandered restlessly for a time. When he returned to Aleppo, he was told that another man – could he be a kinsman, however remote? – of the same name, Bernard, had died there. At once our Mr Bernard wrote to Mr Gordon, who now wrote to me this extraordinary, almost incredible, tale. I read it with a renewed sense of tragedy, of the cruel irony of fate: the book found that proved her innocence, her delusion, her husband alive and on his way home – and the poor lady utterly crazed and lost in mind.

At once I wrote to Mr Gordon a full account of my visit to Redcleugh, of my discovery of the book and of old Andrew's narrative. He replied that he was coming to Redcleugh, with the Laird, to whom he had told all the tale. Would I join them? This I was indeed bound and eager to do.

Mr Bernard brought his children with him. And he sent the little lass, Mary, into her mother's room, by herself. I had counselled him not to appear himself, suddenly, fearing the shock to my patient. The child ran in. There was a wild scream, and Mary rushed out again, sobbing. Then Mr Bernard took command. He walked into the room, went straight to his wife and took her into his arms. 'My poor wife, my love, forgive me.'

She was silent, looked up into his face and fainted. We summoned the cook, laid Mrs Bernard on a sofa and ministered to her. I was now hopeful; a swoon can be a signal of natural, healthy shock, and so it proved. My patient came to herself and looked up into the loving eyes of her husband, who spoke to her very lovingly again. She broke into sobs and gasped his name, and the name of her child. She was truly herself again. It was as if a black shadow had lifted and vanished.

Then all went well. The two bairns came in, Mary still timid, but her mother welcomed her with such tenderness, smiling to her, that she was reassured.

It has been a long tale I have told, one very near tragedy. The happy ending came quickly. Mrs Bernard recovered in mind very soon; she was, after all, young and healthy in body, and love and happiness are a fine elixir. Next day I departed, giving my promise to return when they desired.

I thought much about those two dear and beautiful ladies on whom a curse had fallen. It was lifted now, and it seemed to me, after much meditation, that each had taken it in her own way. The Lady Lillah had borne it with Christian courage, as the martyrs for the faith had borne their suffering. She had made an offering of it to the Saviour Who suffered for all men, and surely now she was, as old Andrew had declared, in bliss. Amelia had endured even worse agony, but that agony was expiation. She herself was innocent, but she had suffered the burden of guilt and now it was lifted. There would be no more darkness about the house of Redcleugh.

Old Andrew had wept, that day of release and rejoicing. 'Och, Christy, my dear, would ye were alive to see this day. But meybe ye ken – aye, and the Leddy Lillah too. Mebbe your prayers an' hers ha'e helped to bring this aboot.' And I think he was right.

My next visit to Redcleugh was not as doctor but as guest to the most welcoming of hosts. It was summer, and house and garden were full of light. The children were lively and joyful. Andrew had brought back some of the old servants, and the place was in perfect order and comfort.

We dined, the Bernards and I, in the evening sunshine. It was an excellent dinner; but the deep rose-red wine of Burgundy, old and noble, that we drank with it, would have made a bannock and cheese into a banquet.

Source:
J. M. Wilson and Alexander Leighton, *Tales of the Borders*

Elfland

Elphin: Cup-bearer to the Fairy Queen

The belief in fairies lingered long in the Borders, and especially in Annandale, by Corrie Water, a deep, mysterious river. They were usually known as 'the Good People', beautiful and merry, dancing on their green hill, playing enchanting music which often lured mortals away, young men and girls, drawn by a fairy lover into that kingdom beyond or within this world. Sometimes they did not return; sometimes they came back after what had appeared to them a brief, happy visit but which by our reckoning had lasted for scores of years.

Two of the most cheerful and most popular young people in the countryside were Phemie and Elphin Irving, twin sister and brother. They were nineteen years old, and for three years had been orphans. Their father had been drowned in Corrie Water, while trying to rescue one of his sheep, and their mother had died of grief. Once their initial grief was over, they lived happily together, both much sought-after. They were cheerful and pleasant in manner; they were musical and loved dancing. Many a lad lost his heart to Phemie, many a lass hers to Elphin, but neither responded with anything warmer than friendliness.

They led a peaceful life, tilling their land and herding their sheep. Elphin would sometimes drive the flock to pasture on the hillside over the river, when the water ran low and clear.

Phemie would spin some of the wool and weave it to make a cloak for him.

One summer evening she was sitting by the river, waiting for him to return with the flock. It was late, and dusk was falling, clear dusk with stars glimmering in the sky in gentle radiance. Suddenly a light flashed more dazzling and less serene, and a shadowy figure approached the river on the opposite bank. There was not a sound to be heard. The figure leapt across the water and went into the cottage. Phemie followed, ready to greet her brother and to prepare supper and ask about the flock, but there was no one there. The poor lass shrieked and fainted.

She was found next morning by a neighbour, lying in a chair half conscious, waxen white and still as if frozen.

'Phemie, lass, what ails you? Whaur's Elphin?' The neighbour rubbed the cold hands and held the chilled girl in her warm arms. Slowly Phemie came to herself.

'There, my lass, lie still and I'll bring you some hot milk. I fear I have some ill news. Yestreen Corrie Water rose to a flood, and this morning seven o' your sheep are drowned. But the flood has sunk again, and my man says he'll gang wi' Elphin to rescue the rest o' the flock. Here's yer milk, lass. Drink it and bide still. Dinna fret owre sair aboot the sheep.'

'But whaur is Elphin?' asked Phemie wildly. 'I saw him yestreen come owre the water when it was low and still; he seemed to go into the cottage, but when I followed there was nae sign o' him. There was a bricht licht in the sky, I saw him plain – or was it his phantom, no' himsel'? Och, I see it clear. He's been taken by the Good People. His true self is wi' them. He has sent his likeness to warn me, to bid me seek and find him and bring him hame.'

The neighbour tried to comfort poor Phemie, and she put her to bed, bringing her food and drink. She went home and told her husband, who went out with some of the neighbours to look for Elphin and his flock. The sheep were found, but not the shepherd, although every man and boy in the place searched hill and fields and river banks. The water now ran clear and still. They could see down to the depths and could bring up the drowned sheep, but there was never a sign of Elphin.

'Drowned like his faither, puir lad,' said most people.

'He is not drowned, he is not dead, he has been taken,' Phemie declared. 'He came to warn me. I'll bide here and welcome him when he comes.'

Before long she was up and about again, active about the house and the fields, herding what was left of the flock, very quiet, as if she were waiting for something.

Rumour spread like wildfire, and there were plenty of folk who believed that the Good People had stolen Elphin. Some of the older folk thought that there was fairy blood in the twins' veins. Others declared that the Good People would not be able to hold him for long. Many prayed for him and for Phemie, and neighbours helped her in the work of the fields. More than one kind woman would have come to live with her or taken her to live with a family, but she would have none of it. 'I maun be here when Elphin comes.'

One old wife recalled the tradition that once in seven years the Good People must pay tribute to hell, that the prince of evil came himself to demand a victim and that the People tried always to have a mortal to offer him. 'Noo they'll send Elphin and nane o' their ain. The time maun be near.'

A night came of wild wind and rain. A farmer was riding home late, well happed up in coat and plaid, but even so he felt the deadly cold. As he rode near the river by Phemie's cottage, he saw a white figure which at first he took to be a ghost. Then he saw that it was Phemie herself, standing by the water, singing a strange song: a lament for Elphin, a plea to the Good People to send him back.

She sang of the elves and fairies riding with their Queen who had lured Elphin away, as she had lured many another before him, to be her cup-bearer – as indeed she had once lured a forebear of theirs. He had returned eventually, but only after many years, and he was never the man he had once been. Now Phemie implored the Queen to release Elphin, before he could be that tiend they paid to hell, before he could change.

The farmer halted his horse and dismounted. Phemie saw

him and ran to him with a cry of joy: 'Elphin, ye ha'e come back!' Then she fell in a swoon.

The farmer wrapped his plaid about her and carried her to the nearest cottage. And there, early next morning, came two herds carrying another body, that of Elphin, whom they had found drowned in a deep pool of the river. One of his hands was still clutching the wool of a sheep he had been trying to rescue.

But Phemie knew nothing of this. The last flicker of life had left her body as she lay in the cottage, and soon brother and sister were laid together in one grave.

They were long remembered in that countryside. Their story was often retold round the fireside, though no one knew just what had happened. Had Elphin indeed been taken? Had Phemie seen his fate? Had the death of his body brought the release of his soul? It can never be known. They can only be remembered with compassion and prayer.

Source:
Allan Cunningham, *Traditional Tales of the English and Scottish Peasantry*

Alice Learmont

'What hae ye dune, you misguidit lass? Bringing' ill luck on the bairn sune to be born?' The formidable Dame Learmont glowered at her daughter-in-law, Marion, whose time was very near. 'Hangin' the cradle wi' green ribbons, the colour the Gude People like and that brings little gude to mortals. Forbye, ye're a Graham yersel', and green is unlucky for the Grahams.'

'I thocht only to mak' the auld cradle braw,' pleaded Marion. She had brought out the old cradle that had held many generations of Learmont babies, had polished it, furnished it, made white curtains to hang in front of the deep hood and tied those curtains with gay green ribbons just to brighten them up. Had they been blue or cherry or rose red, there would have been no reproof.

'Ye maun mind,' the Dame went on a little less sternly, 'that the Learmonts are no' a' thegither canny. Yer ain man, my son Tammas, is in direct line frae Thomas the Rhymer, True Thomas wha rade awa' with the Queen o' Elfland; he cam' back after seven years, but no' to bide. She summoned again, sendin' a hart and a hind to fetch him, and awa' he went wi' his harp and ne'er again was seen by wife or weans or ony friends. Nae grave hauds him noo.'

Marion listened, worried and not a little frightened. There was nothing fey about her own man, Thomas. He was a good husband to her, and kind; but she was often anxious, for he was quick tempered and had some enemies – among them one

Graham, a kinsman of her own who hated him, it may be from jealousy.

'I wish Tammas wad come hame,' she said.

'Ach, it's mirk and misty. Ye can hardly see the Eildons. An' it's Hogmanay, a nicht when the Gude Folk are aboot and ha'e power.'

The Gude Folk, the Gude Neighbours, the Other People – all these were ways of referring to the fairies whom few cared to mention by that name, for that might attract their power or their mischief. It was well to placate them by courteous words.

Suddenly a voice could be heard singing outside.

'It's daft Simmie,' said Dame Learmont. 'Hearken!'

The voice sang words that many a ballad-singer had sung about a rider who did not return:

> Hame cam' his saddle a' bluidy to see,
> And hame cam' his gude horse, but never cam he.

There was the sound of galloping hooves, and the two women peered anxiously out of the window just in time to see Thomas's horse arrive riderless at the stable door.

'So he has been killed,' said his mother with the calm of one who had foreseen the worst. Marion stood without a word, white as a sheet. A moment later a servant lad rushed into the room.

'The horse is in a sair fricht, but there's nae blude on the saddle, and naething has been taken. The purse the maister had is still there. He's been ta'en awa', no' killed by mortal haun.'

'Aye, the Gude Neighbours will be abroad this nicht,' said the dame. 'And my son bears the name o' his ancestor, Thomas the Rhymer, who went awa' and will ne'er come back.'

Again the voice of Daft Simmie could be heard singing:

> There were twa lads fechtin' on Eildon hill;
> With a hey and a ho and a hoodie-craw;
> The ane the ither's blude did spill;
> Ho! Ho! says the hoodie-craw.

The poor young wife fainted. Her pains came upon her, and she was carried into her room. At the very hour when the old year yielded to the new, the baby was born, a wee girl. 'Alice,' the young mother murmured. It was the name of her own mother, a gentle, loving woman who had died a year and more ago. Dame Learmont and a servant lass did all that was needed, for the birth had not been at all difficult. The maid went back to the kitchen, and the new-made granny washed the baby and laid her in the cradle, still decked with the green ribbons. There were sounds from the courtyard, and the tramp of feet of men walking slowly, bearing a burden. The dame looked out: 'They are carryin' a body – God grant it's no' oor Tammas. I maun go and see.' She went out quickly, leaving the door ajar.

The young mother lay half in dream, part sorrowful for her husband, part joyful for the birth of her daughter. 'Alice, wee Alice,' she murmured. 'Oh, Tammas, come an' see oor bairn, Alice.' Her mind was half in a dream, but her senses were very keen. She heard and saw everything very clearly; there was the sound of many voices – light, soft and merry – and a host of tiny figures, girls in green gowns, boys carrying quivers of adder-skin with reed arrows; and among them was one who was taller and lovelier than any, wearing a crown of gold and diamonds. Well did Marion know that this was the Queen herself, the Queen of fair Elfland who had long ago taken True Thomas away and had now come for his descendant, the new-born baby.

She spoke to Marion very sweetly. 'Let me have your daughter. She will be happy with us. You are poor here, and there we are rich. I promise you I shall let her come back to you, if she will, for a visit a year from now on her birth-night; and afterwards every seven years – if she will. Let me have her, let me have your wee daughter.'

Still barely conscious, Marion lay murmuring her baby's name: 'Alice, wee Alice,' and the Queen heard it with joy for to know and speak a name gives power.

'Give me your daughter Alice,' she said. An attendant scooped the baby out of the cradle with its green ribbons. There was more laughter, and the fairy host began to drift away, taking the baby with them.

Dame Learmont came back. 'They ha'e brocht back Graham, wounded and drooned. They found him in the Tweed. Daft Simmie saw oor Tammas an' him fechtin', an' baith fell into the river. But o' Tammas there was nae sign there, up or doun the Tweed, though they searched weel. I kent it. He's been ta'en awa' and God alane kens will he ever come back to us. God help us, and the new-born babe – whaur is she? Whaur is oor wee Alice? They ha'e ta'en her too.'

The dame was not given to tears, but now she wept sorely. Marion lay very still as if frozen with grief.

The Queen and her company mounted their horses and rode away. By the river bank they stopped to talk to the kelpie, a fearsome creature with green skin, grey-green shaggy hair and eyes colder than the coldest water.

'I have him and I will hold him,' he boasted. 'He lies deep down there, sound asleep.'

'You may have him for a year,' the Queen told him sternly. 'Then you must send him to me, for that will be the seventh year when we must pay teind to hell, and I must have a mortal man to give.'

'Ye hae the auld Rhymer,' grumbled the kelpie, 'an' ye ha'e this bairn.'

'I shall never let my Thomas go,' answered the Queen, 'nor this child either; at least not yet a while. See you obey me.'

The kelpie sank down into the depth of the river, grumbling angrily, but he dared not disobey. The company rode on, back to their own land and halls. There the baby was fed on fairy food and milk from fairy cows. The Queen touched her with her wand, and from a baby she grew into a most lovely little girl – not little by elfin standards, but much bigger than a human baby, and walking and dancing on feet so light and swift that they might have been wings.

A year passed – by our reckoning, for in that other country it is different. The Queen told Alice she might go to the river, and off she went on dancing feet, flitting about beside the water almost like a fairy herself. In the river lay the figure of a man, and on the bank stood another: this was a very tall man who spoke to Alice – not in the fairy speech she knew but in a strange tongue which somehow she understood. As he spoke, the man in the river awoke, stirred and moaned: 'Lat me gang, lat me gang back to my ain country, to my bonny wife. Oor bairn maun be born noo. Lat me gang, lat me gang.'

The tall figure on the bank looked at him with compassion.

'Had I but had your mindfu', faithfu' he'rt, I'd ne'er ha'e come here again, I'd ne'er have been held in thrall. I loo'ed my wife and bairns but no enough. The Queen's spell was stronger, so I am under thrall, and I'll ne'er return to Ercildoune.'

The man in the river heard and answered. 'Are ye indeed my great forebear True Thomas, that went awa' and didna' return? It's a puir place we ha'e noo at Ercildoune. The fair ha' is but a ruckle o' stanes, and we bide in a cottage, but we are happy, Marion and I, and I am fain to return to her.'

Thomas the Rhymer spoke sadly. 'Aye, the prophecy I made has come true – wad that it hadna.

> 'The hare shall kittle on my heart-stane,
> There'll ne'er be a Laird o' Learmont again.'

The man in the river wept, and there were tears in the Rhymer's eyes. Alice flitted about, uneasy, bewildered. Tears were strange to her, as to the Other People, who dreaded them.

The Rhymer turned to her again, and said: 'My bairn, ye ha'e heard and understood. I speak in mortal tongue, in the speech o' Tweedside, like yer faither – for he that lies below there is yer faither. Ye hear noo he longs to return to his ain place, his ain hoose, his wife and a' he holds dear. This nicht brings yer ain birthday – a year since ye were taken awa. Ye may return noo to see yer mother. Will ye gang?'

'What will it be like?' asked Alice. 'What is a faither? And a mother?'

'Ye may sune see. The Queen has lifted the spell that hauds ye here – but only for an hour, so gae noo quickly yonder whaur ye see the lichts.'

Alice flitted away like a bird, almost like a fairy. The Rhymer stood looking sadly at his descendant, who lay weeping in the river. Alice was back, like a flash of light.

'I have been there. I have seen her, my mother. She just sits and weeps. I don't like it. I am afraid. And her house is cold and dark and small. I would rather stay here.'

'If you will stay, your faither may return. Thomas, my son, I shall speak to the Queen. She is coming now.'

The Queen came riding by with her cavalcade. The Rhymer bent low and went on one knee before her.

'Lady, I implore you, let this man go to his own home. His daughter does not want to leave you.'

'So you have chosen, Alice,' said the Queen. 'You will not leave us for your mother?'

Alice looked troubled for a moment. Then the splendour of the Queen and of her cavalcade enfolded her, possessed her. 'I will stay,' she said, and the Queen looked triumphant.

'Then let this other fellow, your descendant, go back to his poor home, my Thomas,' she said. She bent down to touch the man who lay in the river. The Rhymer stepped into the river to lift him out, and the younger Thomas struggled to his feet. He looked bewildered – and looked with gratitude at his ancestor; then he leaped across the river and went with great strides towards the lights of Melrose.

Marion and her mother-in-law were sitting by the fire, both sad, for the past year had not brought them much joy. Suddenly there was a knock at the door, and a dear voice they had not hoped to hear again called out: 'It's mysel', Tammas. Will ye lat me in, my love?' There he stood on the threshold, his very self, unchanged, a glow of love and joy on his face as he caught Marion in his arms.

'Sae ye've come back,' said his mother dryly. 'I thocht mebbe ye would, but I wasna sure.'

'Thanks be to God! He has set ye free,' said Marion, in tears of joy, but also of longing for their lost child.

'Saw ye ocht o' wee Alice?' demanded Dame Learmont.

Of that young Thomas's memory was shadowy and confused; of all that had happed in that year of exile he remembered little or nothing, for he had been held in enchanted sleep. Now at last his normal human life took over, and happiness returned to the home – though Marion thought constantly of her baby girl and prayed for her return.

In that other country Alice grew in beauty – a strange, ethereal beauty, with an elfin touch to it. In this other world seven years went by, and once again it was Hogmanay, and

Marion sat by her fireside. The dame had died a year or so before; she had greatly mellowed in her old age, telling Marion what a good wife and daughter-in-law she was, and a gude mother to the three boys born in those years – Hugh, Sandy and Habbie. The three were sitting on stools by the fire. Thomas was away, for he had been made one of the Queen's Archers and was on duty at Holyrood where Queen Mary was spending Yuletide and the New Year.

Suddenly there was a sound outside, faint at first, a knock at the door, a little voice calling: 'Let me in.' Hugh ran to open, and there stood a little girl, very lovely; she was almost of elfin beauty. Marion rose and looked, bewildered at first, then with joy of recognition: 'Is it you, my bairn, my Alice? Come in, my lamb, my bonny wee lass!' And she caught Alice in her arms. 'It's yer ain sister I've tauld ye o',' she said to the three boys, who stood staring in amazement. 'And they're yer brithers,' she told Alice. The boys were shy and silent; they had indeed heard much of their sister who had been taken away, but they did not speak much of her.

Marion sat with Alice close in her arms. The child grew restless, so her mother set her down and went to prepare supper. She set the table with bowls of porridge and milk, and the children took their places at the table.

'Say grace, Hughie,' his mother bade him, and Hugh spoke the good words of thanks to God. Alice stirred and shivered a little at the Holy Name. 'That hurts me,' she said.

The boys supped their porridge with good appetite, but Alice soon put her horn spoon down, for it was poor, rough fare for one who had fed on fairy delicacies and fruit and had drunk fairy wine. She leapt to her feet. 'I will go back now,' she said.

But her mother caught her and held her close. 'Bide wi' us, my bairnie, my wee previous lamb. This is yer ain hame and these are yer ain brithers.'

'Ah ye bide wi' us, we'll ha'e graun ploys,' Hugh begged. 'I'll tak' care o' ye. I'll no' lat Sandy and Habbie torment ye.'

'Yer faither will be hame sune and blythe to see ye. We'll all love ye weel, my ain wee lass, Alice.'

'What is it, to love?' Alice asked. For reply, Hugh kissed her. She took it coldly but did not push him away.

The night wore on. 'Time for beddit bairns,' said Marion softly. 'Next Hogmanay mebbe I'll lat ye sit up, Hughie, to see the New Year in.'

The three boys went off to bed, after kissing their mother and (very shyly) their sister. Alice shrank back just a little; she did not return their kisses, but she accepted them. Her mother sat by the fire, holding her close, not speaking. When midnight was very near, there were sounds from without, the hooves of little horses, fairy steeds, voices, laughing and alluring.

'Alice, Alice, come with us. It is time. There is feasting in the hall; there is dancing, and there are minstrels.'

Alice stirred in her mother's arms. They could not take her, those other people, for the door was closed. Only if it were opened to them would they have power.

'Bide wi' us, Alice, my love, my bairn,' murmured her mother. 'Let me bar the door.'

She set Alice down.

'Oh, it is cold, cold,' cried the child. 'I must go back. I want to go back.'

She ran to the door and opened it, and the voices called joyfully. She ran out and the fairy host swept her away. There was a feast awaiting her, with music and dancing. At home her mother sat weighed down with grief, and next morning her brothers cried.

Time passed on earth; in elfdom all seemed lovely and timeless, but Alice began to weary of the cold splendour as her human blood grew warmer within her, and she began to think less of the poverty of her mother's cottage than of the love she had found there, something strange and never known in Elfhame. Earth was calling her just as that other country called some humans, her own ancestor among them. The years passed on earth. Alice grew into a beautiful young lady, still with a touch of elfin loveliness, but she was taller than any of the Good People, taller even than the Queen herself. She began wandering about that realm, restlessly, and came one day to the river where her father had been held. And there she saw the kelpie, ugly, evil, boasting of a new captive. She looked into the green water, and there she saw her brother Hugh. Had he been taken? Had he come looking for her?

Thomas the Rhymer was suddenly there beside her, tall and grey and gaunt, his harp over his shoulder. He played a tune, not of elfdom but of Tweedside, and Hugh awoke and began struggling towards the bank. The kelpie screamed out in fury: 'He's mine. I'll haud him for the Queen.'

But Thomas was the stronger, and soon Hugh stood beside his sister on the bank.

'Stay with me,' she begged, 'and I will show you all the marvels of fairyland.'

But Hugh was like his father, steadfast and loyal. Nothing would persuade him to leave home.

'Let him see some of the splendours,' Thomas said, 'and see whether they attract him. But remember that the seventh year has nearly come, the year when the teind must be paid to hell. He came here to seek you.'

Alice led her brother about the glamorous kingdom, but for him it held no allure. 'I maun gang hame!' And True Thomas urged his departure. Alice gave him to wear in his bonnet a fern plucked on earth on St John's Eve which would make him invisible to the kelpie, to any of the elfin folk. She led him on the long, long way that their ancestor True Thomas had ridden with the Queen, so long ago; over desolate plains, up and down stony hills, over rivers red with blood shed upon earth. At last they came to the great stone door. Alice bade him look through a slit between the door and the door-post.

'What do you see?'

'I see the sun on the Eildons. I see the lichts o' Melrose, the licht in the Abbey.'

Alice touched the great door, and it swung open, just a narrow chink.

'Haste ye, Hugh. It will close again soon.'

'Come wi' me, Alice. Come hame wi' me!'

'I canna. I was ta'en awa' an unchristened bairn, and they ha'e power o'er me' – and how she knew that, and how she suddenly spoke in the good, homely speech of her own country she could not tell, but perhaps True Thomas had put the knowledge into her.

Hugh slipped out, and the great door clanged shut behind him. He sat on the snowy hillside and wept for his sister. Then he ran home, to the great comfort of his mother and father.

The time drew on to Hogmanay upon earth. Marion sat alone, sorrowful. Her Thomas was at home now, and the sad Queen Mary had been taken prisoner and was held in captivity. Thomas was busy farming some fields and herding some sheep and cattle. He was poor but content, and the boys were a tremendous help to him on the land. But Marion seemed only half alive, pining and longing for her daughter.

Suddenly she saw a face at the window, a face she knew, and heard a voice plead: 'Let me in, Mother, let me in!' and her strength came back to her. She rose and opened the door to receive Alice in her arms. They clung to each other for ages, and for the first time in her life Alice shed real human tears.

'Oh my bairn, my ain wee lass, ye'll bide noo.'

'Fain wad I, but they'll come for me.'

And they came. They could not enter the house, but a great host of them gathered outside, summoning Alice, commanding her in the name of their Queen.

'I maun gang,' said Alice sorrowfully. 'I am compelled.'

'God will protect you, my bairn. He will not allow you to be lost. Gin ye canna come to me, I will come to seek ye.'

Then the mother remembered something very wonderful. At Roodmas, on the eve of the finding of the Holy Cross on which Our Lord won salvation for all mankind, the fairies ride. And if any mortal have courage to enter their realm and to wait – as once Janet waited for her love, Tamlane – she may save a mortal held in their power.

Alice knew all about that, for True Thomas had told her.

'I shall come then and bring you home,' her mother promised. And outside the clamour grew. Mother and daughter clung to each other. Marion made the sign of the cross on Alice's forehead. The poor lass opened the door and was caught up and swept away remorselessly. Her mother wept, but not without hope.

In elfdom Thomas the Rhymer met the daughter of his earthly house. He had pleaded for her, but the Queen was merciless. In great compassion he took Alice to the river, where he sprinkled her with water and signed her with the sign of the cross: the words and the rite came back to him.

'Alice, I sign thee with the sign of the cross, and I baptize thee in the Name of the Father, the Son and the Holy Spirit.'

And with that, new sight came to Alice. The glamour of elfdom faded and dissolved. The splendid hall was a ruckle of stones; the tapestries became withered trees, the rich carpets fallen leaves. The golden tables and seats had turned to toadstools; the silk curtains were spider's webs. Small, ugly creatures flitted about, and on a tree stump for a throne sat the ugliest of all – an old crone whom Alice had seen as the Queen. She shrank back in horror, but True Thomas stood by the tree, for he was still in thrall.

On earth the spring returned, and the trees put out green leaves. One evening a willow branch came floating down the river – the sweet branch used on earth on Palm Sunday and in Holy Week. The blessed feast of Easter was near, and on earth there was much joy. In elfdom on the Eve of Roodmas, in May, the fairies rode in a long cavalcade, with the Queen at their head. The glamour seemed to invest them all again, but for Alice it held no allure, no truth. All the same she was compelled to ride, last of all in that long procession.

That night her mother came, crossing the river, wearing a cross, murmuring prayers and uttering the Holy Name. She waited till she saw the cavalcade, with the Queen, proud and beautiful, and Thomas riding beside her, silent, enthralled. At the very tail end of the procession rode her daughter Alice.

Thomas bade her farewell. 'I shall never return to earth, but I implore you to remember me and have Masses said for me, so that my soul may yet be saved.' Alice promised. Her mother would know what to do.

Marion crouched down under some bushes. She was wrapped in a dark cloak and hood, and the splendid procession rode past without seeing her. When Alice came, her mother leapt up, and with a strength she had never known before she seized her daughter, dragging her from her horse and holding her close in her arms. She found she was holding a fierce wild beast, but Alice had warned her of this, and she remembered the old tale of Tamlane and his faithful, fearless love, Janet.

She held on firmly and would not let go. The beast changed to a snake and to many another loathsome shape, but still the mother held fast. The last shape of all became a living flame. 'Save us, Lord! Save us in body and soul!' cried Marion, and suddenly she found herself holding no fearsome shape, no flame of fire, but her own warm-blooded daughter, safe in body and in soul.

By this time the procession had turned to bare branches, and there was not a sign of Queen or fairies, only a sad voice bidding them farewell. 'God bless and save True Thomas,' Alice murmured.

Together they went home that holy eve, through the soft gloaming of a warm summer sky.

In the windows of the abbey lights glimmered, and from the chapel came the sound of voices singing. It was early morning of Holy Rood Day, and the monks would soon be singing Mass.

Mother and daughter went home – to Thomas and Hugh, Sandy and Habbie, and a great welcome. That day they went to Mass and gave thanks to God. That evening they heard a voice singing and a wandering figure passed: it was Daft Simmie, who had not been seen for many years. Some folk said that he was involved in Alice's capture by the Other People, but this could not have been true. Be that as it may, there he was now, singing gaily:

> Summer and winter baith come roun';
> Spak the mither to her bairnies three;
> Tint was tint, and found is found;
> I'll hap my heid saft in my ain countrie.

Source:
Dinah Maria Mulock (Mrs Craik), *Alice Learmont*

Will o' Phaup

There have always been those who have from time to time a
sight of the Other People which may be terrifying and is always
uncanny. One of such men was Will o' Phaup, Will Laidlaw,
grandfather of James Hogg, the Ettrick Shepherd, who, if he
had not the sight himself, had a heritage beyond that of most
men.

Will too was a shepherd, on the farm of one James Anderson
of Phaup. In his prime he was known and admired for two
qualities: his swiftness as a runner, and his store of songs and
jests, and, it might be added, his capacity for good French
brandy. Once he was set to run against a champion who had
never yet been overtaken and who appeared elegantly turned
out in ruffled shirt and well-fitting breeches. Will wore his
rough working clothes. He was reluctant to take on the contest
but was persuaded. His rival ran off like a hare; Will followed
at his swiftest. Just as he was near coming up with the other,
the string holding up his breeches broke and the breeks fell
about his feet.

'There was I, standin' like a hapshekeled staig!' He jumped
out of the breeks and, running on like a stag, came up with his
rival. 'I scarcely kenn's whether I was touching the grund or
fleein' in the air.'

He heard a friend who was standing by say exultantly:
'Phaup has him yet,' which was true.

Just before the goal, Will leapt ahead. 'I got by him.'

Another time he was set against a famous English runner. The bet, fixed by his master, was the price of three hundred wedder hogs. Will won, to the farmer's great delight. He rewarded Will with a guinea, a pair of new shoes and a load of oatmeal. With this award Will was very well satisfied. It meant as much to him as the three hundred hogs to his master.

Will was greatly liked and welcomed in every farmhouse and cottage in the countryside, for his songs and his jests. But there was another Will besides this entertainer and swift runner. He was the last man in that region to have seen the Other People.

Will lived in a lonely shieling on the edge of Ettrick Forest, far from any village or from other cottages. It was the last refuge of those People who were being gradually banished by the force of preaching by the Kirk. They were reluctant to depart; they lingered in lonely places. Will had a glisk of them sometimes by moonlight or in the summer twilight, riding on their tiny horses, in long procession.

Once he saw them sitting on the green grass at the foot of a deep ravine. They were feasting and drinking their own rare wine from cups of silver or gold, no bigger than a harebell. They heard him move and looked up at him with neither fear nor menace in their brilliant blue eyes, rather with a touch of pity for this poor mortal who knew nothing of their joys.

Another time he heard a great chattering and laughing, as if from a throng of children. Following the sound, Will crept very quietly over the grass to the edge of a rocky precipice. It was still daylight, with a glimmer of sun in the sky. Down at the foot he saw a company of ladies, sitting round their Queen. They too were feasting. At the back of the company two maids were baking fine white loaves to be eaten as they came fresh and warm from an oven. They sat on green grass which had never grown there before. Will looked very cautiously. He laid his broad bonnet aside, but he made a slight sound, and from the laughter that floated up he knew that he was seen. He heard them speak his name. He was not greatly afraid for it was still day. Then he remembered that this was Hallowe'en, when the Other People have power and the spirits of the departed are about, before the day of All Hallows when the blessed saints protect mankind. Will knew that, if those little people spoke his name thrice, it would be a spell to bind him. In panic fear he fled, very softly, home to his family. He shut fast the door, gathered his children about him and fell on his knees in prayer. But he did not tell them until many years later what he had seen and heard.

Another time he was riding home late from the fair at Moffat. He was alone, and the night was dark and full of shadows. Will heard voices, laughing and talking, although he could make out no words. Ahead of him he could see shadowy figures. He rode faster, hoping to come up with some company, but they kept always ahead. Then he called out: 'Neighbours, what news o' the fair?'

There was silence, then laughter, then more chattering, but still he could make out no word. He rode still faster but could not come up with them.

'Bide, neighbours, bide till I come up with you,' he shouted. 'Tell me your news o' the fair.'

Again silence, again mocking laughter, then a voice spoke: 'Ride hame, ride hame, Will o' Phaup, and luik to yer ain hearthstane.'

Will spurred his horse to a speed he had not reached before. The people ahead had all disappeared. There was silence but for the sound of hooves. He came home full of foreboding, but all was well. There was no hostile or fearsome thing on his hearthstone. But there might have been.

All these encounters happened in his prime. But when he was old and alone, his wife dead, his children scattered, he had the strangest meeting of all.

He was sitting on a green knowe beside his cottage one evening when three tiny boys, all exactly alike, came to him.

'Gude e'en to you, Will o' Phaup.'

'Gude e'en to yersel's, ye bit craiturs. Whaur are ye for, the nicht?'

'Nae further nor here if ye will give us food and shelter.'

'Siccan scraps as you will need but little. Come awa' in, and welcome. Whaur dae ye come from?'

'From a place ye dinna ken. We ha'e an errance to you.'

'Come awa' then, and tell it, an' tak' yer bite and sup.'

Will walked into his kitchen, followed by the three scraps. He went to his cupboard to fetch food and drink.

'An' what's yer errand?' he asked, without looking round.

'We are sent to fetch a silver key that you have.'

In utter amazement Will cried: 'A silver key! In God's name whaur cam' ye from?'

He looked round. The three tiny boys had disappeared.

Will's encounters happened to him alone. But one experience had, if not immediate witnesses, at least witnesses at one remove.

Again he was returning home, late and alone, from the fair. His way led past a hill. Looking up, he saw a bright light at the top. He had never seen one there before, and from impulse and curiosity he began to climb the steep, rocky slope to a great cave in the rock which he could not remember having seen before.

The entrance was wide enough to let a man crawl in, though very low. Crouching down, he looked in and saw two men moving some brandy casks, bigger than usual, about the rocky floor. At the back stood two huge barrels. As Will looked, one of the men turned and came towards the door: a man of great height and width of shoulder, with grizzled hair and a shaggy, grizzled beard. He seemed to be staring directly at Will, who was terrified, but the man took no notice of him. Will had seen more than one smuggler about, but this was none of them. The cave was clean and dry enough, but the casks had a mouldy look as if they had stood there a very long time. The huge man came nearer. Will slithered away, then fled, running, leaping, falling down the rocky slope faster than he had run any race. He reached home exhausted, thankful to be safe.

Next morning he told some of his neighbours what he had seen. There was some chaffing. They told him he had been putting away too much brandy, but they did not mock or disbelieve him. He was well liked and respected for his honesty. They accompanied him to the hill and, as they climbed, saw trace of his ascent and downward rush. Will led them to the place of the cave – but there was no cave there. Yet near it were traces of horses' hooves, recently made – and Will had not ridden his horse that night.

They no longer doubted or queried his tale. Strange things had happened in that countryside, among those hills, and might well happen again. The mystery was never solved.

Source:
James Hogg, *The Ettrick Shepherd's Tales*

The Good People, The Good Neighbours

'The Good People' and 'the Good Neighbours' are terms of propitiation used of those Other People, elves, fauns, fairies and brownies. They can also be true. These others do not forget. They exact punishment for any injury done by a foolish mortal, but they can act with gratitude and be rescuers.

It happened like that to Sir Godfrey MacCulloch in Galloway. His was an old house with deep foundations and a subterranean cellar never used or entered by him or his household. It was not, however, unoccupied. One day as he was out riding, he was met by a little old man with a long white beard, dressed in green and mounted on a white horse.

'Good day to you, good neighbour,' said Sir Godfrey courteously. The term was truer than he realized.

The little man answered: 'We are well met, Sir Godfrey. I am in a sore plight.'

'What ails ye? Is there anything I can do?' – he was a kindly man, as his tenants and servants knew. He would always listen to any plea.

'I bide doun there, below your hall and hearth, in a place ye never visit. It was a fine bield, but noo the filth frae yer drain and sewer is flooding in and I'm fair scunnert.'

'That maunna be. I'll see to that, guid neighbour,' Sir Godfrey promised him; and he did, without delay. The drain and sewer were deflected and repaired, the flow of filth stopped. The Laird thought no more about it.

He was a kind man and friendly, but he was also quick-tempered and quick on the draw. A quarrel with a neighbour ended in a fight, and Sir Godfrey killed him. He was taken, tried and condemned to death. Between his trial and the day of execution he lay in prison in Edinburgh, in the Tolbooth. His family and friends made a plea for him: he had acted in haste, in the heat of temper, under provocation. But the plea was not granted.

The scaffold was erected on Castle Hill. Crowds began to gather early in the morning. The prisoner was led out. He walked quietly between his guards, while the crowd looked on with pity. As the procession reached the foot of the scaffold, a horse came rushing through the crowd, a white horse with a rider dressed in green: a little man with a long white beard.

'Mount, Sir Godfrey,' he called, and the prisoner, who was not manacled, broke from his guards and leaped up behind the rider – the horse rushed off, the crowd falling back, and neither horse, little man nor Sir Godfrey was ever seen again.

Source:
Sir Walter Scott, *Minstrelsy of the Scottish Border*

Love and Grief

Helen of Kirkconnel

I wish I were where Helen lies,
Day and night she on me cries,
I wish I were where Helen lies
On fair Kirkconnel lea.

The haunting poem tells of faithful love, of cruel jealousy, of revenge.

Kirkconnel lay on the banks of a small river, the Kirtle, in Galloway. The Laird and his wife lived happily there with their only child, a daughter called Helen, who was the bonniest lass in all that countryside, and as good as she was bonny.

She was poetic in mind, a dreamer, spending much of her time reading some of the old poems and romances of which her father had a good collection; in summer she loved to sit by the river bank or in the wood. The quiet life led by her parents, who had not been young when they married, suited her very well. There were not many young folk in the neighbourhood, and no eligible young man, but that was no grief to her. She had her dream lover, out of romance; her world was the world of stream and fields, woods and flowers, birds singing in the trees. Her true love, if he should ever come in the flesh, must understand and love that world of hers.

That was all very well for a time, but her parents would have liked to see her betrothed to a real lover. So they welcomed a kinsman, Walter Bell of Blacket House not far from Kirkconnel, when he visited them on several occasions, and at last he asked for Helen's hand in marriage. He was indeed the Laird's next of kin and so might be his heir and join two branches of the family.

He was not the ideal lover likely to captivate a girl's heart. Most people found him dull, reserved, even morose in manner, and some muttered worse things: he was said to have more than a streak of cruelty in him, to have taken part in the recurring battles between those two great families the Crichtons and the Johnstones, and to have killed some of the latter; and this not out of kinship or friendship with the Crichtons but from sheer sadism and possibly also a certain amount of self-interest.

But Helen's parents knew nothing of this, and Helen herself neither welcomed nor rejected Walter. He was far from being her ideal lover, but who could be? Her only difficulty of choice would have been between Sir Lancelot, Sir Tristram, Sir Galahad and Sir Gawain. Walter could be agreeable enough when he chose, and he chose now; he made some effort to show interest in Helen's love of books and of nature and to walk with her in the woods. She knew she must marry someone sooner or later, and if this pleased her much-loved parents, it ought, perhaps, to please her too. Walter was only too ready to accept any encouragement. He began, indeed, to show a demanding passion which startled and repelled the shy girl. Whether or not she would have withdrawn altogether from this betrothal will never be known. What is known is that another lover appeared on the scene who awoke Helen from both dream and uncertainty, who made Walter appear of no account and even made Sir Lancelot, Sir Galahad, Sir Tristram and Sir Gawain recede into a dim background.

Young Adam Fleming of Kirkpatrick was one day hunting a doe within the Kirkconnel lands. In its flight, the creature swam the water and fled into the woods where Helen was sitting in her bower, reading her favourite romance of Sir Tristram. The rush of the doe startled her. She rose and looked after the lovely creature, then saw before her a youth who might have come out of the romance itself. Adam was tall and handsome, strong and gallant, courteous and friendly. He bowed to Helen with a few words of apology, introduced himself and begged forgiveness for having invaded her solitude. For both of them it was love at first sight. And Helen, in spite of (or perhaps because of) her dreaming innocence, had instinctively chosen to love wisely and well. Young Fleming was of excellent family and reputation, but until then he had cared little for girls, nor shown any thought of matrimony.

To her delight Helen soon discovered that he was a lover of poetry and romance almost as ardent as she herself. The deer was soon forgotten as they sat together and talked, and before parting they arranged to meet again. That was not difficult, for Helen was given to solitary walks, to withdrawing into her bower with a book. Adam was very fond of riding and spent long days out of doors. He was of a good family, much respected, but there was one difficulty. In the recurring feud between Crichtons and Johnstones, the Flemings had supported the latter. Would Helen's father overlook this? Would he consent to a new suitor for his daughter? He might be persuaded, for he loved her dearly and would think of her happiness. But Walter was by no means easy of temper. He was not likely to relinquish his bride even if he had never held her heart.

For the moment they lived in a rapture of love. With every meeting they loved each other more. But both knew it was unsafe, for at any time Walter might come upon them as he knew well where Helen loved to walk. He had gone on a visit to some kinsfolk but he would be back before long, and Helen's father expected to arrange the wedding date soon after that.

Beyond the wood lay an old kirkyard, no longer used for burials and hardly ever visited. There they used to meet at dusk or by the light of the moon. The Kirkconnel household kept early hours, and the Laird and his wife went early to bed. So no one asked any questions when Helen retired to her room to read.

One night when the moon was almost full, she waited until all the house was quiet and her own maid had departed for the night. Helen wrapped herself in a long, dark cloak and slipped out by a side door. She walked swiftly and silently over the

lawn and through the wood to the old kirkyard where her true
love was awaiting her. For an hour or so they were happy
together, then Helen came silently home, into the house and up
to her room. They had several secret meetings like this, and
Adam urged Helen to let him speak to her father, to risk his
displeasure and Walter's jealous anger. Or should they flee
together?

One night when the moon was just on the wane, Helen sat
by her window. There was still a lovely silvery light, as the
clouds drifted across the sky. It was very still outside, not a
sound, not a movement – yet whose was that shadow? It
retreated. It must be one of the servants returning discreetly
from the inn or from a visit to his sweetheart, or perhaps some
young fellow had come hoping to meet one of the maids. Helen
thought indulgently of any other possible pair of lovers. She
waited, but there was no further sign of life outside.

Wrapped in her cloak, the hood drawn closely over her
bright golden hair, she slipped out by the familiar way, crossed
the lawn and hurried through the wood to the old kirkyard
where the dead slept in peace. They would do her and her lover
no harm. She found Adam sitting upon a green mound.

'My dear, my love, what has kept you?'

She told him about the shadow. 'But I am sure no one has
followed me. It must have been someone slipping quietly into
the house.'

They kissed and clung together, sitting on the green mound.

'Helen, my dear love, I must speak to your father. I will not
carry you off, and we cannot go on meeting by stealth. He can
have nothing against me, except that my family are allied to the
Johnstones, and who cares now for those foolish old feuds? Let
me speak to him, then let me take you to my mother and father,
who will welcome you. You are not finally betrothed to Walter
Bell, so you are breaking no promise.'

Helen was a little afraid. Her father could be quite set in his
ways, and she was more than a little afraid of Walter, whose
jealous and passionate temper she had begun to see in flashes.

'Wait a little. Let me speak to my mother and father when I
see a suitable moment.'

So after an hour or so Helen went softly and swiftly back as

she had come, into the house by the little side door and up to
her room. Was there a shadow again across the lawn?

She slept and awoke resolved to speak to her parents. But
when she came into the parlour, she found Walter there with
them, and grim and dour he looked. Could he suspect? Was it
even possible that he might have followed her? He glowered at
her but said nothing, beyond a surly word of greeting. But he
continued to look at her with that sullen glower.

The day passed gloomily. There was menace in the air as
Helen walked out, followed by Walter. He spoke very little. He
no longer pretended to show any interest in the scene, in
anything she might care for, and she could take no refuge
anywhere.

Her mother came to her and gently and lovingly begged her
to accept Walter as her betrothed and to have a date for the
wedding announced.

'He is dour, I know, my darling; he is not easy to get on with,
but he loves you and he is an honest man. Your father and I are
growing old, and we would see you settled before we die.'

Her father too begged her to consent to the marriage. He
might have commanded it, but that was not his way, and the
very gentleness of her parents made it all the more difficult for
Helen to bear. But she knew now that she could never marry
Walter. Even if she had not met Adam, she would have been
afraid of Walter, and with Adam waiting in the wings she
found Walter strangely repulsive.

She tried to put things off by pretending to be ill, and indeed
she was exhausted and far from well. She was convinced now
that it had been Walter's shadow that had followed her
through the woods that night. Now that he knew, he would be
sure to take vengeance upon Adam. What would happen she
could not guess, but clearly she could not keep up the pretence
of illness for long. What must be done was to warn Adam, to
bid him go away and stay away and make no attempt to see her
for a while.

The moon had waned, and the nights were dark. The new
moon rose, pale and slight, and grew to fullness. Adam would
be waiting for her; she must go to meet him and warn him.

This time there was no shadow by the door or on the lawn.

Helen wrapped herself in her dark cloak and slipped out, through the garden, over the lawn and through the wood, till she came to the old kirkyard. Adam was there, her brave, true love. Helen warned him that he must go, but he would not listen.

'I shall never leave you, my love. You must not return to your father's house. You will come with me. My horse is ready, and we can ride to safety and be married and spend the rest of our lives together.'

They held each other closely.

From the darkness of the wood a shot rang out. Helen fell. The bullet meant for Adam had pierced her heart. Adam laid her gently on the ground and rushed to find the murderer. Walter had no time to flee, so he turned and drew his sword, at the very moment when Adam drew his. But it was Adam who struck first, and Walter fell dead on the spot. Yet Adam struck again and again in a frenzy of despair.

> I hackit him in pieces sma',
> For her that died for me.

Then he returned to kneel by the body of his love until men came seeking her in the morning.

Adam lived for only a little time after her. Death was welcome to him, lifting the sore burden of his grief. Death came mercifully also to the old Laird and his wife. Adam's love and faithfulness passed into a ballad.

> O Helen fair beyond compare,
> I'll mak' a garland o' thy hair
> Shall bind my heart for evermair
> Until the day I dee.

Source:
J. M. Wilson and Alexander Leighton, *Tales of the Borders*

Lord William and Lady Margaret

It all came from the harshness and tyranny of a father who would not let his daughter marry her true love. There may have been some family feud, or it may have been possessiveness, for the lover, Lord William, was gallant and honourable, and he and Lady Margaret should have been joined in happy wedlock.

'Wauken and rise, Lord Douglas. Rise up if ye would not have your daughter carried awa' by Lord William. Rise up and ride.'

The warning voice awoke Lord Douglas. He arose and called loudly to his seven sons: 'Wauken and rise. Rise up and ride. Ye should ha'e ta'en better care o' your sister. She's awa' with her lover, Lord William, and ye maun overtake them and bring her back. Ye ha'e lain too lang asleep.'

The seven sons did not lie long after that. They were up and dressed and armed. They mounted their swift horses and rode after the lovers before she and Lord William had ridden very far.

She rode her milk-white horse, he rode his grey. They went swiftly, but the brothers were beginning to come up with them. Lord William looked over his shoulder at the sound of galloping hooves.

'They are coming, my love, your brothers and your father leading them. They are armed and ready for the fight. Dismount, my love, and hold your horse and mine while I go to meet them.'

Lady Margaret stood holding the milk-white mare and the grey. Lord William went to meet her brothers and her father. They fought fiercely, and so well did Lord William defend himself that he slew them one by one, leaving only her father, who was badly wounded.

'Oh, hold your hand,' Lady Margaret cried. 'Spare him my father dear. Other lovers I can find, many a one, but only one father, and I love him dearly.'

She left the horses and came to kneel by her father, wiping the blood from his wounds with her handkerchief. But his wounds were deep, and his heart's blood flowed, redder than any rose, redder than wine.

'Choose now,' her lover said. 'Will you ride wi' me or bide here yer lane?'

'I'll ride wi' you. There is no choice.'

He lifted her on to her milk-white steed and mounted his grey, and they rode on in the light of the moon until they came to the wan water of a stream.

'Light down, light down,' said Lord William. 'I must drink of the wan water for I am parched with thirst.'

They lighted down, knelt and drank. And as Lord William stooped, the lifeblood from his wounds stained the wan water red as wine, red as the blood that had flowed from the heart of Lord Douglas.

'My love, my love, you are sore wounded. Your blood flows fast.'

'It is only the shadow of my scarlet cloak that you see in the wan water.'

They mounted again and rode on and on, in the light of the moon, until they came to his mother's door.

'Rise up, rise up, my mother dear, rise up and let us in. For I ha'e brought my bonny bride who will be daughter to you.'

His lady mother rose and let them in and embraced her son and his bride.

'Make now our bed, mother dear, and make it wide and deep. If Lady Margaret lie at my back, then soundly I shall sleep.'

The bed was made, both wide and deep, and the lovers lay down to sleep. And Lord William was dead before midnight, Lady Margaret by break of day.

They buried Lord William in St Mary's Kirk, Lady Margaret in the choir. Out of her grave grew a red, red rose, and out of his a briar. They grew and they twined together as the hearts of those lovers had twined, as their lives would have twined if cruel death had not come.

And may all true lovers be happier than they.

Source:
Sir Walter Scott, *The Minstrelsy of the Scottish Border*

The Two Sons

There is more than one tale of lovers parted, broken in heart, coming to death together through the cruelty of a harsh father. The story of Lord Graeme and Sir Robert Bewick tells of paternal pride and jealousy breaking the friendship of their sons, forcing them into enmity. In their way they were good men up to a point, and good friends – until the boasting of one humiliated the other, whose revenge for that hurt was mean and base.

They lived, Lord Graeme and Sir Robert, on opposite sides of the Border, and one day they met in Carlisle and proceeded to celebrate their meeting. They went to an inn to drink good wine, drank merrily and deep, to their long friendship. Then Graeme proposed that they drink to their sons.

'Gude lads they are, baith o' them. Gude sons and gude frien's like you and me.'

'Aye,' said Sir Robert Bewick. 'But your son is not so good as mine. I sent him to the school and he learned his books; he is a fine scholar. If your son had learned like that, they would have been like brothers. But you sent your son to the school and he would ne'er learn. Ye bought him books which he would not or could not read.'

Lord Graeme glowered at his companion, who now did not seem his friend. He spoke in anger: 'My son shall ha'e nae blessing frae me till I see him defend himself against yours.'

He rose, paid the bill, went out to the stable to saddle his horse and rode away, back over the Border, brooding over the insult, muttering in wrath.

When he came home, his son met him with cheerful greeting. 'Whaur ha'e ye been, sae lang awa'?'

'I ha'e been at Carlisle wi' him I thocht my frien', Sir Robert Bewick, an' his son I thocht was yours. But he says ye canna be equal comrades ony mair, for young Bewick's a scholar and ye're nae guid at a'. Sir Robert sent him to the skule an' he learned his books. I sent ye and ye couldna learn. He bought his son books an' he reads them. I bought ye books an' you canna read. Ye maun defend yersel' against young Bewick or ye shall ne'er ha'e my blessing.'

'Faither, Faither, God forbid that I should fight wi' him my comrade, my master. I am but his pupil.'

'Haud yer tongue, silly loon that ye are. There is a quarrel noo between Sir Robert and mysel', and it is for you to mend it, gin ye can. If ye winna fecht young Bewick, ye'll fecht me, yer faither. There, by my glove I swear it.' The glove dropped from his hand.

Young Graeme stooped and picked it up. 'Faither, put on yer glove again.'

'What say ye, base loon that ye are? Daur ye answer me sae? I've tel't ye, I tell ye again, if he dinna fecht wi' young Bewick, ye'll fecht wi' me.'

The poor lad went to his room, to think and to speak to himself about the dreadful choice.

'If I kill my dear comrade, I shall never again have the blessing of God. If I kill my faither, I commit mortal sin. If it must be that I kill my comrade, then so be it. But I myself will be the next to die.'

He put on breast-plate and helmet, took sword and buckler, mounted his horse and rode over the Border to find his dear comrade.

Young Bewick had been tutoring some boys in fencing and the handling of a sword, and now he was walking in his father's meadow. He carried his sword under his arm. A man was riding rapidly towards him, his armour bright in the sun.

'Who is that? Why, it is Christy Graeme, my comrade, my

brother. Christy, Christy, you are welcome. Dismount and walk with me.'

'I'm no' welcome, for I come, wae's me, on a sair errand. I maun fecht wi ye. My faither compels me. Dark was the day my faither met yours at Carlisle, an' your faither said I was useless, bad at my books unable to learn, no' like you wha's a scholar. My faither says I'll ne'er ha'e his blessing until I avenge the insult. If I dinna fecht wi' you, I maun fecht wi' him and that wad be mortal sin.'

'But that must not be, Christy, my comrade. Never can you and I draw sword one again t'other. Let us each choose three good men to go to our fathers and make peace between them.'

'Alas, that canna be. We maun settle it atween us wi' the sword. So cast off yer cloak and come owre the dyke and let us fecht and ha'e dune wi't.'

'But I have no armour.'

'Nor ha'e I, noo.' Young Graeme threw down his shield and cast off his breast-plate and helmet. He leaped from his horse, tied him to a tree and stood unprotected, holding only his sword. Young Bewick leaped the dyke, threw off his cloak with a psalter in the pocket which he had been reading, and stood, facing his comrade, sword drawn.

For two hours they fought, thrust and parry, their sweat falling in great drops but never a drop of blood, until a backward thrust by Christy pierced young Bewick under his left breast, and he fell, his heart's blood streaming.

Christy threw down his sword and stood by him.

'Speak to me, oh speak. Let me tak' ye to a surgeon who'll heal ye. Tell me ye are nae wounded to death.'

'Alas, dear Christy, Christy my good comrade, I am dying. You are not guilty. Our fathers have done this: theirs is the guilt. Take horse, Christy, and fly, before any can come and see you. Then none will know who dealt this blow for I will never tell.'

Young Christy Graeme said never a word. He thrust the hilt of his sword into a molehill, drew back a score of paces, ran forward, leapt above his sword and fell on the blade. There he lay dead, beside his dying comrade.

Sir Robert Bewick came up, panting with haste and with fear.

'My son, my dear son, you are alive, and young Graeme is dead. Rise up now, for it is you who are the victor.'

'Not I, not I, Father. You might have held your proud, foolish tongue. Your boasting has brought us both to death, and we will soon be together again. Now dig my grave and make it wide, that Christy, my comrade, my dear comrade, may lie with me there; and bury him on the sunny side.'

'Alas, alas, the greater loss is mine,' lamented Sir Robert. 'I have lost the fairest son that ever man had. Mine is the loss beyond all other.'

Then Lord Graeme came riding up furiously and heard his words.

'Na, na, mine is the greater loss, the loss beyond all ither. Mine is the lack. I could na'e ridden the Border through wi' Christy my son at my back. Had I been ta'en, and led through Liddesdale, thirty horsemen guardin' me, Christy my son would ha'e set me free. I've lost my hope, I've lost my joy, I've lost the key to every lock. I could ha'e ridden the wide world through, if Christy my son had been at my back.'

Source:
Sir Walter Scott, *The Minstrelsy of the Scottish Border*

The Lass of Lochroyan

'O who will shoon my foot, and who will glove my hand? And who will gird my waist with linen and who will comb my golden hair with silver comb? And who, O who, will be father to my new-born babe until Lord Gregory come home?'

Fair Annie, the lass of Lochroyan, held her baby in her arms, murmuring over him.

Her father answered gently: 'Och, I will shoon your foot, your mother will glove your hand, your sister will gird you with fair white linen, and your brother will comb your golden hair with silver comb. And God Our Father will be Father to your bairn until Lord Gregory come home.'

But Annie would not wait.

'Let me have a boat to sail,' she begged, and a boat was fitted out, a strong boat, with silken sails and a mast of gold. 'I will not wait. I will go to find my love, if my love will not come to me.'

She took her small son in her arms and went aboard the fair boat. The sails were hoisted, and she sailed away over the waves.

They met a robber with his band. 'Are you the Queen?' he asked, and he bent his knee for he was a courteous man, though a rogue. 'See you yon tall tower, bricht in the sun, built on a high rock? Yon is Lord Gregory's dwelling. Sail now round the rock and gang to the tower and call him, Lord Gregory, your love.'

The robber sailed away. Fair Annie's boat sailed on, round the rock and the tall, bright tower. The sailors threw the anchor; they carried fair Annie, her bairn in her arms, to the shore, and she walked up to the fast-locked door. She looked up at the window and called to her love: 'Wauken, Lord Gregory, wauken and rise. Come doun and open the door to me, your true love, and our bonny bairn.'

But no answer came from within the high tower. She knocked and called again: 'Rise up, rise up, Lord Gregory. Rise up and let me in, your true love Annie and our bonny bairn, your son.'

But never a sound came from within. Then at last Lord Gregory spoke, and his voice and his words were hard and cold.

'Awa' wi' you, ye ill woman. Ye'll ha'e nocht of me. Ye're here for nae guid. Ye're no true woman. Ye're witch or mermaid frae the sea.'

'I'm neither witch nor mermaid. I am your own true love. I ne'er lo'ed anither, and this is your ain bairn, your son. Hearken to me, my love, open the door and tak' me in.'

'If ye're Anne of Lochroyan – an' sair I doubt it – tell me some token that passed between us.'

'The first token that passed atween us was the ring that you gi'ed me and that I gi'ed you. Yours was a bonny ring o' yellow gowd, but mine was bonnier. It was the clear diamond. Mind ye no' that we changed them as we sat at supper, drinkin' the guid red wine frae a silver cup? And then, Lord Gregory, my love, my dear, I gi'ed ye a token and a gift faur beyond gowd or diamond. I gi'ed ye my maidenhood. Ye took it frae me as we sat on the green hill. Lord Gregory, my dear, my only love, open to me and let me in, me and the fair son I ha'e borne ye.'

But still he answered coldly, sternly: 'If ye be truly Annie o' Lochroyan, tell me mair o' the tokens that passed atween us ere I let ye in.'

'If that be your answer, I'll speak thus: may no woman who bears a son ever be so full of woe as I this day.'

She went down to the sea and was carried to the fair ship.

'Brak' the gowden mast. Tak' doun the silken sails. Put up

a mast o' wood and sails o' canvas. My he'rt is broken, and it is no' for me to sail like royalty.'

Her sailors obeyed her, and the ship sailed away. The sea was high, the winds rose lashing it, and the brave ship broke and sank.

Lord Gregory awoke, weeping sore. He rose and called to his mother: 'Mither, Mither, I ha'e dreamed an ill dream: that Annie, my love, my dear, cam' to the door wi' oor fair son in her arms and cried to me to let her in. Then I dreamed anither dream, Mither, Mither, an ill dream: that bonny Annie o' Lochroyan, my dear, my love, lay dead and cauld at my feet, our fair son in her arms. Mither, Mither, did ye drug my wine? Did ye put a spell on me. Are ye a witch and nae true woman, Mither, Mither?'

He opened the door and went down to the edge of the cold, cruel sea. The wreck of the boat tossed on the waves. Annie, the fair lass of Lochroyan, lay there on the shore, cold and dead. The bonny babe was no longer in her arms. The wee body had been sucked down beneath the strong, cruel waves.

Her lover stooped over her. He lay upon her, clasping her, kissing the lips once cherry red, now cold and white. But no breath stirred. Her golden hair drifted wet as seaweed; her face was white as the foam.

Lord Gregory knelt, weeping.

'O woe is me, that have lost my love, my dear. Woe to my mither, that fause evil woman, and an ill death may she die. For she turned my dear love frae my door, my true love that had come sae far to seek me. Ill befall you, Mither. Evil be your death, you who drove my true love from my door who came for love of me.'

Source:
Sir Walter Scott, *The Minstrelsy of the Scottish Border*

Jellon Graeme and Lily Flower

She was more fair than the lily of her name. She was gentle and loving, too loving and yielding, for she gave herself to Jellon Graeme, in whom was no gentleness at all. He cared for none but himself. He took what he desired and would not pay.

When Lily Flower's time was come, Jellon called his page. 'Ride you now, swiftly, to my lady's bower, and bring her here to me.'

The page rode swiftly though not willingly, but he dared not disobey. He came to the lady's bower at daybreak before the sun rose and called up to her window: 'Are ye asleep or are ye waukin, Leddy Lily Flower? We maun ride to Silverwood. But I doot sair if ye'll ride hame again.'

The lady leaned out from her window.

'I'll come, I'll come, though I'm near my time. This verra day may see my bairn come to birth. But Jellon Graeme bids me come. He may well desire to have his son born in his own house.'

She came down, wrapped in her cloak. The page took her up behind him. Swiftly they rode in the dawning light until they came to a grave newly dug, and from it climbed Jellon Graeme, Lily Flower's lover, the false lover, drawing his sword.

'Licht doun, licht doun, Leddy Lily Flower, for ye'll ne'er ride again.'

The poor lass fell on her knees weeping.

'Spare me, oh spare me, Jellon my love. By our love, I pray

you, and by our babe so soon to be born, spare me. Let me gang into the green wood, and I'll bide there wi' my bairn, and nane will ken.'

But the cruel false lover thrust her pleading hands away.

'It is for that bairn ye maun die. I daurna let ye live. Your faither would slay me, and my ain life is dearer to me than yours or the bairn's.'

The poor lass knelt weeping. Then the pains of childbirth seized her, and there in the greenwood, beside the newly dug grave, her son and Jellon's was born.

As she lay there in her pain and weakness, Jellon Graeme pierced her to the heart with his sword. He ordered the page who stood by, trembling with fear and horror, to help him lay her in the grave. He thought for a moment to lay the new-born child in her arms and let him die. Then he paused. Here was a fair son who would live to do him honour. He ordered the page to fill in the grave above the poor body that streamed with heart's blood.

'Gin ye tell this to onyone at ony time, ye will be deid as the corpse that lies there.'

The boy obeyed. Then he fled, shivering and sobbing.

Graeme picked up the new-born child and rode to the home of his own old nurse to whom he gave the bairn, ordering her to find other women to help to tend him.

'See that he is never left alane by nicht or by day. Should ony harm come to him, there'll be waur harm for you.'

The woman took the child. She found others to help. It is said that there were nine of them: three to care for the child by day, three by night, three to relieve them. He was nursed well and tenderly and no word was spoken. It was safer so. No vengeance was taken, for Lily Flower's father was old, and she his only child left. He died of grief, not knowing where she had gone, whether she was alive or dead.

When the child had grown to boyhood, strong and brave and bonny, his father came for him and took him home, declaring that he was his nephew, his sister's son, his sister having married in some far-off place, and now dead. Whether or not that was believed, none dared question it. It was safer to be quiet.

The boy grew in his father's house. He learned to ride, to shoot a straight arrow: he always carried a bow. One day Jellon Graeme and he came through the greenwood to a green mound. Primroses grew there and early white lilies and roses red as blood.

'What bonny flowers,' said the boy. 'I ne'er saw so many nor so sweet.'

Jellon Graeme spoke without thinking: 'Your mither was the fairest flower and the sweetest, sweet as the primroses, white as the lilies, red as the rose. Her name was Lily Flower, and she lies there beneath the green knowe. Redder than any rose was the blood that ran when my sword pierced her through.'

He came to himself like a man recovering from a dream. But it was only for a moment that he stood there, for his son moved back, fitted an arrow to his bowstring and drew. The arrow flew straight and pierced the evil heart of the murderer.

'Lie there, Jellon Graeme, whom I will never call my father. Lie there for the corbies to pick, for the grave that holds my mother is too good a place for you.'

Source:
Sir Walter Scott, *The Minstrelsy of the Scottish Border*

Fause Foodrage

There was a lovely lady once, gentle and good and valiant. Many wooers, kings and nobles, sought her. One desired her for her dowry, another for her lands: but one, King Honour, who was worthy of his name, wooed her for love of herself, and she gave him her love in return. They were married.

They were happy – but only for some short months. Though most of his people loved their good King, there were some rebels, ill-disposed nobles, eager to seize power.

'Let us draw lots as to which of us will slay the King,' they proposed.

But the strongest, most ambitious and most evil among them, Fause Foodrage, said: 'Nae need to draw lots. I'll kill him mysel' and that richt noo.'

He went, dagger in hand, to the gate of the castle, slew the porter and took his bunch of silver keys. Then he opened the great door, and other doors one by one, locking each behind him, until he opened that of the great room where King Honour and his Queen lay peacefully asleep.

'How dare ye come into my room, Fause Foodrage? How cam' ye here? Whaur gat ye the key?'

'That matters nocht. Ye'll sune ken my errand' – and with a thrust of his dagger he pierced the King to the heart.

The Queen fell on her knees. 'Spare me. Let me live until my time has come and I have borne King Honour's child, be it son or daughter.'

Fause Foodrage looked down without pity. 'Be it a dochter, she may live. But a son an' I'll hang him. He'll be fine an licht on the gallows.' His laugh was devilish.

People mourned for their King, but they dared not rise against those powerful and ruthless nobles, especially Fause Foodrage who would have slain anyone who even muttered a word of rebellion. The Queen was kept close captive. Four-and-twenty knights were sent to guard her. There must always be four outside her room, so that she could not move or cry out for help without being heard. But she was brave and as resourceful as she was brave. She made no effort at escape, made no appeal – knowing well that these young men, unworthy of their knighthood, would have mocked her and that, had they shown her any compassion, left her for a moment unguarded, let any other come to her, they would have paid with their lives.

She had another plan. She sent for wine and ale, much red wine and strong brown ale.

'Will ye drink to me and the bairn that is to be born?' she asked. This they did willingly and drank to excess. Before long they were lying bound in drunken slumber.

'My time is very near,' the Queen said to herself. 'I am indeed great with child. I dare not go out through the doors and rooms; I would be seized – and killed. I will try the window, narrow as it is. Oh, Mary Mother, Lady of Succour, help me.'

Our Lady heard and answered. The brave lass got out by the window. She wandered about the grounds of the castle until she came to the pigsty, and there the pains took her. Alone and unaided (except by Our Lady of Succour), she bore a fine son, there in the straw.

Meanwhile Fause Foodrage had come to change the guard and had found the four silly young men still in their drunken sleep and the lady fled. He made short work of them, and not many tears were shed. Then he called some older knights and ordered them to draw lots as to who should search for the Queen. The lot was drawn by the best of them, a good man well named Wise William. Like a wise man he went to his wife.

'I will gang and search for the puir leddy,' she said. 'We baith were near oor time, and my bairn, oor wee dochter, is safely born and I'm weel. I may be in time to help oor Queen.'

Off she went, carrying her baby, and came to the sty. The Queen rose feebly to her knees.

'Och, madame, what gars ye kneel to me?' protested the good rescuer.

'I kneel to beg you to save my son.'

'An' that I've come to do if I can.'

'Fause Foodrage will spare me but he has vowed to kill my babe if it be a son. Now here is my plan. Tak' you him home with you and bring him up as your own son. Let your good man, Wise William, train him to ride, to shoot from the bow, to draw sword and dagger. I will tak' yer bonny wee lass as my dochter and teach her all a princess should know: to read and write, to do fine needlework in silken and gowden thread.'

Wise William's wife agreed. She loved the Queen, and her heart went out to the tiny boy.

'When we meet at Mass or it may be in the hall,' said the Queen, 'I shall ask you how is your gay goshawk, and you will ask me how is my gentle dove.'

Wise William's wife went home to her good man and told him. He thought well of the plan. Then he and his wife brought the Queen and the tiny girl back to the castle, to be guarded in their rooms. All went as the Queen had planned. Sometimes they met at Mass, she and the good rescuer, and the Queen asked how was the gay goshawk, the other wife how was the gentle dove.

The goshawk, the young Prince, grew into a fine, tall, gallant lad, skilled in archery, a good rider, likely to be a valiant knight – a prince, a king.

One day he went hunting with his foster-father. They rode out above the castle where Fause Foodrage ruled the domain.

'That is a fine castle,' said the boy.

'Aye, an' wi' guid lands around it. An' baith castle and lands should be yours, and they will be yours.'

'But hoo can that be? Fause Foodrage is lord o' castle and domain and a' this land, he's nae kin to me.'

'But ye can slay Fause Foodrage, and it will be nae sin. For he slew your father, that was King Honour, a guid king and true;

he hauds yer mither, oor Queen, captive and winna let ye come to her. She has oor dochter wi' her – like her ain bairn. But you are her true son and the son of guid King Honour and the richtfu' king of this castle and a' this land.'

The boy – the young King as he truly was – listened.

'I vow that I will kill him, this Fause Foodrage, this murderer.'

Wise William gave his blessing – and laughed a deep laugh of joy. As evening fell, the young King rode to the castle, armed with bow and arrow. He leaped over the wall and stood before Fause Foodrage.

'What dae ye here? Hoo cam' ye in?' demanded the murderer.

'I cam' owre the wa' and here's what I'll dae' – and the young King drew his bow and let fly the arrow that pierced the black, evil heart of Fause Foodrage.

Then all went swiftly and well. There was no weeping for Fause Foodrage, and none would draw sword or dagger or bow and arrow to avenge him, for he was hated even more than he was feared. The young King went to his mother's room. He knelt before her and embraced her. Wise William and his wife came to tell the tale – and she to embrace her daughter, a bonny and gentle lass. There was weeping, but the tears were of joy and thankfulness. There were prayers and thanksgiving to Our Lady, the blessed Mother.

The young King bestowed half his lands upon Wise William. And before the year was out, he wooed and married his daughter, whom his brave mother welcomed with tenderness and joy. And good King Honour must have known and rejoiced.

Source:
Sir Walter Scott, *The Minstrelsy of the Scottish Border*

The Banks of Italy

There are false lovers and cruel lovers, but this tale is of the most dreadful of all: the demon lover.

The lady was false, although many would not call her so or think her heartless. Her true love had gone over the sea; he was fighting in a strange land. He had vowed to return bringing her gold and jewels to wear, and more gold with which to buy land and a castle. But a year passed, then another year – and so on until, before the seventh year after his departure was ended, the lady had been wooed and wed and had borne two sons. Then her lover came sailing in a tall, fine boat and called to her to come with him.

'Whaur ha'e ye been, thae seven lang years?' she asked.

'I have been lang awa' but I have kept my word and returned to claim you as my bride.'

'But I'm a wedded wife and have twa fair sons.'

He looked at her with bitter sadness, his eyes brimming with salt tears. 'I have come and for you alone.'

'You need not have come.'

'I might have wed a king's daughter, a fair princess.'

'Then you should have wed that king's daughter – though some think me fair enough too.'

'You are, my love. I had your promise and you had mine. I have kept mine. Now I claim you and you must come.'

'Where would you take me?'

'I have seven tall ships out at sea and a band of musicians to make music for us. I have sailed here alone on the eighth ship, and I shall steer her myself.'

His eyes compelled her with a look she had never seen in them before. She took her young sons in her arms, kissed them and blessed them. By a force more compelling than strength of arm, her lover drew her to his tall ship. There were no sailors on board, only her lover and herself.

'Where are you taking me?'

'I'll show you where the lilies grow on the banks of Italy.'

It was a fair ship with masts of gold and sails of fine taffeta. They sailed out beyond the land she knew. The wind blew and the waves rose high but the tall masts did not bend.

'Oh, where are you taking me?'

He answered again: 'I'll show you where the lilies grow on the banks of Italy.'

He stood at the helm, growing taller and taller, driving the tall ship on. They came in sight of some hills, gentle and green, rising above flowery meadows.

'Oh, what are these pleasant hills? Do we go there?'

'These are the hills of Paradise, where you and I will never come.'

The tall ship sailed on. Her helmsman grew taller and taller till he seemed to touch the top of the masts. They came in sight of a great mountain.

'Oh, what is that mountain so great and so grim, covered with cauld, cauld snaw?'

'That is the mountain of hell, where you and I maun go.'

The sky grew black; the wind rose and blew the silken sails to tatters. The snow fell and the air was deadly cold.

'Whaur are we, oh whaur are we?'

He did not answer. He grew taller yet. With his hand he broke the topmast, with his knee the foremast. He broke the tall ship in two, and she sank beneath the cruel, cold waves.

Source:
Sir Walter Scott, *The Minstrelsy of the Scottish Border*

Binnorie

Jealousy is as cruel as the grave, and more than one tale of unhappy love and sad death has this theme: the demon lover is the most terrible, but a sister can be cruel and vengeful.

Two sisters sat in their bower above the river and the mill-dam of Binnorie. Sometimes they spun fine wool; sometimes they did fine needlework in gold and silver thread; sometimes they sang and played the harp. The younger had the sweeter voice:

> O who will come to us in our bower?
> Binnorie, o Binnorie
> By road or river or meadow in flower:
> Binnorie, o Binnorie.

One day a knight did come riding to their bower. He came from their father's court, with leave to woo the elder sister, to whom he brought gifts: gloves and a ring, a gold brooch and a knife sheathed in silver. But to the younger he gave his heart, and she gave him hers. The elder saw it with bitter rage and jealousy.

'Let us go downstream, past the mill-dam, to the river mouth and see our father's ships come in,' she proposed, and the younger agreed: 'Yes, let us go.'

They came to the shore. The younger girl stood on a rock, looking out for the sailing ships. The elder came behind her, seized her by the waist, so slim a waist a man could have circled it with his two hands, and pushed her into the water.

'Sister, sister, help me,' the poor lass cried. 'Reach down your hand and save me. You shall have my share of our inheritance of land.'

'I care nothing for your land. It will be mine when you are dead. You have taken from me the lover who should have been mine.'

'Sister, sister, reach down your glove that I may hold it so that you may lift me from the cruel, cold water. You shall have him, my dear, dear lover. I will not hold him from you.'

'Devil take me if I reach you hand or glove. I shall have him, your lover. He will be mine alone. Your bonny blue eyes, your rose-red cheeks, your long golden hair will drown beneath the salt sea.'

The cruel sister walked away, home to her father's court. The poor drowned lass drifted in the cold, cruel water, and her body was washed again to the mill-dam of Binnorie, where the miller's daughter saw it.

'Father, father, stop your mill wheel. Something is floating in the stream, a mermaid or a milk-white swan, I canna tell.'

The miller stopped the wheel. He waded into the pool and lifted, in gentle arms, the poor drowned lass. His daughter wept over her. They knew her for one of the sisters of the bower, by her gown of fine white silk girdled with gold, by the pearls on her neck and her long golden hair.

As they looked with pity and wonder, a wandering minstrel came by. He too looked with pity and sadness. He sang a sweet lament and said a prayer of requiem. Then he took the breastbone from the body and made it into a harp; he cut the long golden hair and made harp strings. He went to the court, where he was welcomed and bidden to play and sing to the drowned lass's mother and father, her brother, her lover and her cruel, jealous sister. But it was not his own music he played or his own voice that sang. The music that came from the white breastbone that made the harp and from the strings of golden hair was sweeter and sadder than any that ever had been heard, and the listeners wept – all but the evil sister. Then the voice of the drowned lass sang:

'Oh yonder sits my father and with him my mother dear; my brother too, and beside him my own true love. And there is my sister, false and cruel, who drowned me in the cold sea where the river flows that runs by the mill-dam of Binnorie, o' Binnorie.'

The voice was silent, then sang again:

> Woe to my sister, false and cruel,
> By the bonny mill-dams o' Binnorie.

Source:
Sir Walter Scott, *The Minstrelsy of the Scottish Border*

A Border Tragedy

It could be a Greek tragedy (in the country of myth and legend, the Borders are not far from Greece), Aeschylean: of warning rejected, of doom foreseen and fulfilled, a crime expiated long after the death of the offender. But unlike Greek tragedy it ends with a return of joy, like the light of dawn after a night of mirk and storm.

It happened on both sides of the Border, in Berwickshire and in Northumberland. It culminated at the Fair of Whitsome, a village near Swinton, and near where Till runs into Tweed. There is an old rhyme:

> Said Tweed to Till:
> 'What gars ye rin sae still?'
> Said Till to Tweed:'Though ye rin wi' speed,
> And I rin slaw,
> For ae man that ye droun
> I droun twa.'

It was not by drowning that the deaths came, but the last act was by the river, as the act which led to the tragedy began with the fording of Tweed from England into Scotland. The period was the seventeenth century, that of the war between King and Parliament, although that was of less matter to most Borderers than their own feuds and raids.

At the heart of the tragedy was a woman, Barbara Moor,

whom some thought crazy, even possessed, and whom others found pitiful. But none could help her. Once she had lived with her husband, Jonathan, a prosperous farmer with a great herd of cattle. Their home was just on the English side of the Border. On the other side, in Berwickshire, was another owner of land and cattle, one Cunningham, whose herd, even finer than that of Jonathan Moor, the latter vowed to drive away for himself. He was a strong, fearless, most notable reiver, and Cunningham his only worthy opponent and rival.

He had met Barbara, a bonny lass, with her father at Whitsome Fair. Jonathan loved her then and there and asked for her in marriage. She loved him in return, and her father was willing.

'I like ye weel eneugh,' he told Jonathan, 'but I'd fain see ye wi mair cattle in yer byre and a better plenishin' in yer hoose.'

'That I'll provide,' declared Jonathan cheerfully. 'I'll gae reivin' owre the Border, up to Simprin, to Cunningham's land and byres. He has the finest herds on either side. I'll up and owre Tweed and hame again wi' the lot.'

'An' I'll gae wi' ye,' Barbara's brother, young Duncan, told him.

Then Barbara spoke, as one with foresight, the second sight which she had, though none until then had suspected it, from her Highland mother, now dead. She seemed to grow taller, older, her youth falling from her like a light cloak.

'Do not ride that road, though twice the wealth of cattle were there. You will bring doom and death, and it will not end with one. I see the black clouds around you. Do not ride. The doom will last beyond your day. Sorrow will come upon your grey head, and much blood will flow.'

Her father looked at her. Jonathan listened. He had sense as well as courage and daring. He might well have taken her counsel and given up the raid. Her father would not have urged it; but young Duncan, the reckless one, scoffed at his sister and taunted Jonathan: 'Ye're a saft fule if ye hearken her; she's daft. I'll ride mysel' if you daurna come.'

That Jonathan could not endure. They settled to meet late that night at a ford over Tweed where they would cross, they and their horses, into Berwickshire and so to Simprin.

Jonathan proposed taking two good comrades and bade Duncan do the same. Such men were easily found.

Again Barbara spoke: 'Ride not out this night or any night or you will ride to your doom.' Her voice rose to a wail.

Again Jonathan hesitated, but again Duncan mocked. And so they parted, to meet again, each with his two comrades, at the ford, and so over to Berwickshire and on to Cunningham's land and the great fold where his cattle were herded: scores of them, the finest beasts in the countryside.

It was easy to break down the gate and begin bringing out the herd; but suddenly a man rose from a tower at the other side of the field and began swinging a bell round and round. The clangour rolled and pealed.

'Haste ye,' said Jonathan, and the six men began rounding out the herd. Their bellowing added to the din. Jonathan saw that there was no hope of driving them away and bade his band ride as swiftly as possible to the river and the ford, leaving the cattle. Already they heard the horses' hooves of Cunningham and his men in pursuit. Even young Duncan agreed. But the cattle released were stampeding, and their would-be captors could not easily escape.

Cunningham and his men came nearer. The watcher stood in his tower. Duncan madly drew his pistol and fired. The watcher fell from the tower and lay on the ground.

'Duncan, ye fule. That's the worst thing ye could ha'e dune,' Jonathan told him.

There was wild riding on both sides till they came together, swords drawn, and one of the first to fall, pierced in his breast, was Duncan. Jonathan and his four men formed a strong ring, fighting, defending themselves, but the other side was stronger; one of the men fell, the other three surrendered. Jonathan, confronted by Cunningham himself, fought valiantly, but a sword thrust pierced his horse and he fell, though he did not lose his grip of his sword.

Cunningham too had fallen from the violence of the thrust he had given. Jonathan rose to his knees, crawled, rose to his feet and got away, running until he reached a wood and found refuge among the trees. Then he collapsed in a swoon or sleep of exhaustion – but not for long. He heard, first, dimly through the clouds of swoon or sleep, the howls of pursuit. Struggling to consciousness, he rose to his feet, clutching his sword. The howls grew louder, more terrifying; the moon was up, and the pursuer appeared: a great bloodhound, baying furiously. He leapt and threw Jonathan to the ground.

'But I still kept a grip o' my sword,' he was to tell his sons, years later, recalling the raid and its end. With one hand he seized the hound by the throat; with the other he thrust his blade into its chest. The creature gave one last eldritch howl and collapsed on the man; and again he swooned. But the pain of the wounds and the weight on his body awoke him. With a struggle he threw off the heavy body, rose to his knees, dragged himself upright and somehow got himself to the river, to the ford, and waded over into Northumberland and home.

Barbara was there, awaiting him. 'Whaur is he, my brother, the only son of my mother? He is slain. I have seen his doom. Ye have left him, but the doom is still upon you. Och, Duncan my brother, ye were gallant and fair, but reckless ye were that wadna heed my words or the words of our mother speaking through me. My auld father is broken-hearted, his grey head bowed wi' grief.'

Jonathan was deeply contrite, himself broken-hearted. Whether Duncan were indeed slain or a prisoner he could not tell. Then, not long after, three of the men returned. They brought the news of Duncan's death, though not from the wound he took from his pursuer. The watcher in the tower whom he had shot was Cunningham's own brother.

The three men had been told that they would be released if they would betray his murderer. But there was no need for that, even had they considered it. Duncan himself heard and started up, calling out: 'It was I, mysel' and nae ither, and I fain wad kill yersel', Cunningham.'

'Tak' him up to the tower and throw him doun, him whase shot brocht doun my brither,' commanded Cunningham, and he was obeyed by two of his men. The three who had ridden with Duncan and Jonathan were released and came limping home.

There was lamentation for Duncan, and his father did not live long to mourn him. Jonathan was deeply contrite and, partly in compassion, partly because she still loved him, Barbara kept her troth and they were married.

They had a comfortable house, good lands, good cattle. Life went on as it must do. She bore her husband seven fine sons, the first two and the youngest two, twins. They grew to sturdy youth and young manhood, and Jonathan began to forget, to believe that the doom was ended.

War broke out between King and Parliament, for which Jonathan cared little until he heard that Cunningham and his three sons had come out on the side of the King. So Jonathan and his seven rode out as Cromwell's men, and the two forces met in battle. Cunningham's three sons were killed, and Jonathan's seven, and before the end of the battle he himself was slain. Only his foe, Cunningham, lived.

And for him there was still some comfort. Late in their marriage his wife had borne a fourth son and died in giving him life. Her husband mourned her, but in the new child he found comfort. He had loved the elder three with pride, but for this tiny boy he had a tenderness, almost womanly, he had not felt before. This was his joy, his hope, for whom he would live.

For Jonathan's house there was no such light or solace. Barbara was utterly desolate. The doom she had foreseen was fulfilled.

Again she had warned her husband, as once before. 'Ride not out, or ye will ne'er ride home again. Heed me now, though ye heeded me not afore. Ye ken what befell ye then; waur will befa' noo. I see the blackness gather, and there is blood, mair than was shed afore. Ride not out.'

Again he did not heed her. Perhaps he might, as that other time he did begin to listen until young Duncan taunted him. Now it was his sons. They did not taunt, but they urged him: 'Let us gang; bide at hame yersel'. We're young and strang. We'll ride to the battle an' we'll ride hame again.'

But he would not let his sons go without him. And now they had all taken the shadowed way to death.

Barbara, stricken, demented, left her bien house and went wandering about the countryside. Some pitied her, but more dreaded to meet her, although she did no harm to any. She slept, sometimes, in a hut of clay and thatch, but often in the woods – where, none could tell. Some gave her food; somehow she lived. It was the Highland blood in her, folk said, strange blood. Who had her mother been – a witch, kin to the Other People?

Cunningham's small son was growing into a fine laddie. His father took him everywhere. One day he took him to the fair at Whitsome where he went to buy more cattle. He left him for a few minutes in care of a servant while he went to look at a herd and make a bargain with their seller. The bargain was made, and Cunningham came back quickly – the two had drunk to the deal with only one quaich of ale; Cunningham was a sober man and he would not linger. He came to the place where he had left his wee son – and found no one. Then the servant came along, hurried and anxious. He had gone into an inn with a crony – only, he declared, for a minute or two – leaving the boy safe, and he was not a timid or a foolish child. Now he had vanished, and none had seen him go.

His father searched desperately, asked everyone had they seen the boy. He went beyond the fair, beyond the village, asking frantically. But it was as if the boy had been taken away like a child in legend, taken by those Other People – or by the gipsies. But there had been no gipsies that day at the fair.

Cunningham lived on, suffering in fortitude. He adopted a nephew, a son of that brother who had been shot down from the watch-tower, years ago.

Time passed. When 'seven years were come and gane', as in fairy legend, there came a night of violent storm, fearful winds and rain, intense cold. One of the men came in from the byre to tell his master that an old woman had taken shelter in a shed, an open shed with no protection from wind and rain.

'If she bides there till mornin', she'll be deid, aye lang ere day. It's that auld daft wife I've seen rinnin' aboot. Witch she may be, she is no' canny.'

'Witch or no', we canna let her bide to her deith,' said Cunningham. He took a lantern and went with the man, followed by one or two others. There in the shed lay a figure hardly human, ragged, drenched, wild of look.

'Gude peety ye, whoe'er ye may be. Come in and bide by the

fire till day. An' see that she has food and drink to warm her,' he added to one of the servants.

As he spoke, the woman started up with an eldritch cry: 'Cunningham! I'll ne'er set foot in your hoose or break bread. Ye are an accursed murderer, for it was by your deeds, lang lang syne, that my brither, my man and oor seven sons were killed. Aye and yer ain three fell too. An' noo ye've lost the last o' the flock, yer wee son, late-born. But I'll tell ye this, though no' for yer comfort, that the bairn lives. Whaur, ye will never find. Ye may see him but ye winna ken him, or he you. Tak' that for yer comfort if ye can.'

'Where is he, wumman?'

'That I'll ne'er tell. May the knowledge that he lives add to yer dolour.'

She gave a wild shriek and rushed from the shed, disappearing into the night of storm. The old father came back to his fireside, in deep grief and perplexity.

And here the tale diverges to take in another character: one Sandy Reed, a farmer just over the Border. He, like Cunningham, had suffered the death of his wife not long after the birth of their one child, a daughter whom he had named Anne. His had been a late marriage. His aunt, a woman of strength of mind and character and, with it, of real goodness, had come to keep house. The small Anne was dearly cherished and had grown to be bonny and loving and good.

Sandy was a genial fellow. He liked his dram in good company, but he knew, nearly always, how much he could take. For him a day, two days a week, even at the fair meant good trading and good fellowship. It happened seven years before that he had gone to Morpeth and that was for more than a day or two. He did good business, he met friends, but at last he rode off for home on Dobbin, his good horse. A good horse and a good head are needed after a fair. Sandy was sober or nearly so and rode on cannily until he came to a turn of the high road where a path led across the moor. Beyond that, at no great distance, lay an inn known for its good ale and frequented by some old cronies. They were gathered there, and they gave Sandy a grand welcome. They drank together, a full quaich each, then another — and so until the ale-wife's barrel was empty. Then Sandy took leave of them, mounted Dobbin and began to ride back towards the high road. His head was not so good this time, but Dobbin was steady and trusty as ever and carried his rider on until Sandy, half asleep, toppled from the saddle onto the ground and fell into slumber. Dobbin, kind, canny beast, stood still. Sandy slept, half dreaming that he was home again and in bed, the lamp shining in his room, his little lass Anne come to lie on his breast. Then he awoke to find that it was no lamp but the moon, that he lay on the green grass of the moon and that the burden on his breast was not Anne but a strange child, cold as ice, wailing and crying in misery.

'Guid save us! Whence comes this scrap?' he muttered, scrambling to his feet, taking the child in his arms.

'Nae wunner ye are greetin'. Ye're fair frozen, in yer rags.' The child was a boy. Sandy tucked him under his coat and began shouting. There was no one in sight. He shouted again and again, but the night was utterly still.

'Aweel, I canna let the bairn perish, Dobbin,' he said, and he mounted again, holding the child carefully with one arm. The boy seemed to know he was safe, for he was quiet and fell asleep. Dobbin carried Sandy and the bairn safely home, Sandy wondering what account he might give to his aunt and what she might say.

He told her the truth, which was wise, and she believed him, asking only one question: 'Are you the faither o't?' – and she believed Sandy when he said he was not, that he had no idea of whence the boy came.

She took charge of the child, fed him with bread and warm milk, washing him in warm water and happed him in a shawl and a rug. He fell asleep again contentedly. 'He's a bonny laddie,' said the kind woman.

Next morning Anne welcomed him with delight. She had wanted a comrade, and Sandy had always wished for a son as well as a daughter, a son to bring up and to inherit farm and lands and cattle.

He gave it out, after talking to his aunt, that the boy was the orphan son of cousins who had died in poverty. He had him christened with the name of Patrick, his own father's name, and young Patrick Reed became one of the family, accepted easily. From the first Anne and he were the dearest and closest of friends, and as they grew into their teens they desired to be more than friends. It pleased Sandy well to think of Patrick as son-in-law and heir.

Young Patrick was a true countryman. He loved the horses and cattle, handled them well and was a good judge of stock. He was a friendly youth, too, sweet-tempered, not driven to moods or glooms. But one evening he came home looking troubled, very silent, hardly answering questions. That day he had met a wild, daft old woman who had stopped him, demanding his name. He had seen her before, wandering about. Some said she was a witch; everyone said she was daft, a poor vagrant body.

She had stopped Patrick. 'What is yer name?'

'Patrick Reed.'

'That's no' yer name. Ye ha'e another but I winna tell ye that. Let me see yer haun'. Aye, I canna see clearly but I see this, that ye were born to riches and muckle gear though ye may no' come to possess them. But this I see – that yer faither lives, yer true faither, an auld man, grey and bowed, his he'rt sair – an' weel he deserves that. Ye should be his heir but he's ta'en anither, his nephew.'

She had run off then, into the wood. Patrick had come home. He said nothing of this to Sandy or to Anne, though both knew something had happened.

Whitsome Fair had come round, and Sandy and Patrick were to go. On the evening before, Anne came home from visiting a neighbour. On the way she met the old woman, who bade her stop and took her by the hand.

'Staun' and hear me. I ken ye're to be marriet to the lad that ca's himself Patrick Reed though that's no' his name. Ye maun gang wi' him an' yer faither the morn to Whitsome Fair. If ye dinna, there will be sorrow an' blood. If ye gang, ye will win happiness. Gi'e me yer haun' and yer word to gang.'

Anne, frightened, bewildered but steadfast, gave her hand and her word.

'But ye maun tell nane ye ha'e met me. Tell nane why ye want to gang. The doom is near, but noo may be the end. Dae as I bid ye. Keep silent an' for you an' him the licht will come.'

Anne went home troubled. Her father and Patrick were talking about their business at the fair. Anne begged that they would take her.

'What's got into ye, lass? Ye'er ne'er asked this. There's little at the fair for you. Bide at hame wi' yer auntie. Are ye feart to let Patrick oot o' yer sicht?'

Patrick looked at her. He asked no questions, but he may have guessed something. Anne won her plea and next morning rode off with her menfolk.

There was a great throng of folk at the fair, and herds of cattle, flocks of sheep. Sandy had many acquaintances who welcomed Anne kindly and wished her and Patrick well. The news of their betrothal had spread.

Sandy walked about with a purpose. He was set on buying good cattle, and old Cunningham, who had come with his nephew and his men, had some of the finest. After some chaffering the bargain was struck. Both seller and buyer were well pleased, and they all went to the ale-house to drink to each other's health and to the bargain. Anne joined some friendly women for a comfortable gossip.

The two old men drank to each other, drank again. Both had good heads, but the effect of the ale was to make them boastful about the exploits of their youth. Cunningham kept it up longer. Sandy said: 'I'm thinkin' my ain day is past for the wrestlin' and the swordsmanship . . . Aye, Anne my dear, I'll say nae mair aboot mysel'' – for Anne, hearing their excited, loud voices, had come to her father and whispered a gentle word of caution. 'But I'll back Patrick here against ony man in the Borders.'

'He's nae better than my nephew, if indeed he's as guid,' retorted Cunningham, and they grew irascible.

'Let's set them ane against t'ither,' proposed Sandy, and the two lads stood up and stripped for wrestling. Both were strong and agile, but in the end Patrick proved the better man.

'Try them wi' the sword,' called old Cunningham, and they both stood again opposed to each other, swords drawn. Their blood was up, their tempers were roused, the men on each side shouted encouragement – and soon blood was drawn: not much, but enough to rouse the two bands, and the contest became a real fight, with more and more bloodshed.

'Hech, ye fules. Put up yer swords,' called Sandy, and he ran among them. But a sudden thrust from a Cunningham knife pierced through his heart. He fell into the river, staining the clear water with his blood.

Patrick turned in fury on Cunningham himself. 'Ye ha'e slain my father. You shall not live.'

Then another voice broke in, more terrible than any of the shouts of the combatants. The old wife stood there, wild of look. 'Haud yer haun, young Cunningham. Wad ye slay yer faither?'

Patrick recognized her, as did Anne, who was kneeling by her father's body at the water's edge, sobbing pitifully. And old Cunningham remembered the eldritch creature who had come to his place on that night of storm, who had fled, refusing shelter, and who had told him his son lived.

Patrick dropped his sword. As they all stood, amazed, confounded, Barbara, the old demented woman, fell and died there on the ground.

Old Cunningham embraced his son. For him there was comfort after much grief. For Anne – sorrow and tears for her good father. But youth and love are strong. Patrick comforted her, and their marriage brought peace and happiness in the end. Only the Cunningham nephew was sore disappointed, losing his inheritance. But he had just to put up with that.

Source:
J. M. Wilson and Alexander Leighton, *Tales of the Borders*

Trickery

The Monks of Dryburgh

Some of the monks of Dryburgh kept their vows of poverty, chastity and obedience. Of these virtues perhaps the least popular was poverty, and those who broke the vow could plead that they were not doing so for selfish pleasure or in a spirit of rebellion, as with the other two vows. They had the welfare of the community at heart. What was the sense of being poor when there was wealth to be had without doing anyone any harm or depriving any man of his rights? There were benefactors and well-wishers who only needed to be encouraged to leave lands and money to the abbey, with no loss to themselves and with much benefit to their souls in purgatory. They would have prayers in plenty to speed their way.

There was the old Laird of Meldrum, a devout Christian who led an impeccable life, a friend and already a benefactor to the abbey. He was near his end now, and he had no son for he had never married, and he had no near kin. If he left all his lands and money to the community, none would suffer. He had indeed been encouraged to do just this.

So when the monks heard that he was seriously ill and at the point of death, the Prior and the bursar went in haste to visit him with godly comfort. But almost as they entered his room, the old Laird died. Having prayed for his soul, they looked for his last will and testament, but not so much as a scrap of paper was to be found. This was indeed a disaster! Now some far-out cousin would come and take possession, and there would be nothing to prove the Laird's intention of leaving everything to the abbey.

Then the bursar had a bright idea which met with the Prior's immediate approval. 'That is well thought of. Let us tell the Father Abbot of our idea.'

They told it to the Abbot and the whole community, and every one of them commended the bursar for his astuteness. This was the plan. Let them conceal the Laird's death, remove his body and put in his bed, as if on the point of death, a certain poor man of the neighbourhood called Thomas Dickson, who bore a remarkable resemblance to the Laird.

'We shall offer him a goodly fee,' said the bursar, 'and many a meal in the abbey.'

'To say nothing of our prayers for his welfare here and hereafter,' added the Prior.

So the body of the Laird was carried with due reverence into another room; Thomas was told of the plan and was promised a goodly reward on condition that he kept strict silence.

'Certainly I shall,' he declared solemnly.

He went to bed, and the bursar fetched a lawyer with two of his apprentice clerks from the town, and he and the Prior sat silently by the bedside, with the men of law. Thomas contrived to look wan and weak and to speak in a very feeble voice. He declared himself to be of sound mind and clear intention and to be able to make his signature. Then he dictated:

'Hear me, reverend fathers, and you my good man of law. I hereby bequeath to that honest good man Thomas Dickson, this house and all its plenishing, my lands and estate of Meldrum, my moneys and possessions, having long known him as a most honourable man who has suffered poverty and hardship.'

He added a few legacies – to the servants and to the monks – mere tokens. Then he signed the Laird's name in a shaking hand, groaned and sank back in bed with his eyes closed.

The lawyer took it all down, and his clerks signed as witnesses that all was in order. The two monks sat frozen in horror; at that moment they were nearer death, from shock and rage, than Thomas, who was indeed in remarkably sound health. But they could do nothing. They were caught in a web of their own weaving. To denounce Thomas would be to give themselves and the community into the hands of the law. If they admitted the deception, Thomas indeed might be punished for his fraud and cheating, and of course deprived of the legacy which he had made to himself, but that would be nothing at all compared with the scandal that would fall upon the community.

The lawyer departed, taking the will with him. The good monks, he supposed, would stay with the dying Laird until the end, administer the last rites and see to his burial. The lawyer would then inform this Thomas Dickson of his good fortune.

What passes then between Thomas and the monks will never be known. The old Laird was buried with due rites. Mass was said for the peace of his soul, and Thomas requested that another be said, for which he would gladly pay.

The will was not disputed; Thomas took possession and lived for many years in comfort. He was careful to pay the servants all their legacies, and the monks also. And every year, on the anniversary of the old Laird's death, he had Mass said for the soul of his benefactor.

Source:
J. M. Wilson and Alexander Leighton, *Tales of the Borders*

The Gay Goshawk and
the Gallant Girl

Fathers can be harsh and unreasonable and break the hearts of their daughters. But some daughters have the strength of will and of wit to out-manoeuvre their fathers and, literally, to get away with it – that is, with escape to happy marriage. To pretend to be submissive is not a bad idea. In this happy story it worked, thanks to the help of the gay and gifted and loyal goshawk.

Lord William spoke to his gay goshawk, and the goshawk spoke to him, for the bird had the gift of speech as well as of song.

'What ails ye, master dear, that ye are sae thin and wan? Ha'e ye lost sword and spear at the tournament?'

'Na, na, my bonny goshawk, my sword and spear are at my hand. But I pine for my love, my dear love, Lady Jean, who is owre the Border, and her father vows he'll ne'er let her wed me or let me see her mair.'

'Can I no' tak' a letter?' asked the gay and bonny and kind goshawk.

'Ye can, and ye can fly swifter than I can ride.'

'How shall I know your love?'

'She is the fairest of all her sisters. Her skin is white as the down on the sea-maur; her lips are cherry red, her cheeks like a rose. You will find her bower by the birch that grows by the door. At the hour of Mass she and her sisters will come out to go to the kirk, and four-and-twenty ladies with them. They are bonny, all of them, but my love is fair beyond compare.'

Lord William wrote his letter and tied it under the goshawk's pinion. The brave, bright bird flew off swiftly, over the Border into England, to the bower where the birch tree grew. There he lit down and sang a sweet, low song. The ladies came out to go to Mass, and indeed Lady Jean was the fairest of them all, white of neck and breast, red of lips and cheeks. For her the goshawk sang as he had never sung before.

He sang a low, soft note, he sang loud and clear, and aye the burden of his song was: 'Your true love canna win to you. He lo'es you weel. He waits for you. He canna come to you.'

Lady Jean listened and understood. She went to Mass and came back with the other ladies, and they all sat down to dine. The goshawk sang outside the window, sang a sweet and clear compelling song.

'Eat well, my maidens,' bade Lady Jean, 'and drink a cup of wine. I must go by myself to listen to that bonny song.'

She stood by the window; then, as her ladies ate and drank and talked among themselves, she heard the goshawk say: 'Come doun to the door, Leddy Jean. Come doun and let me talk.'

She went softly out of the room, down to the door. 'You come from my true love. Have you a word for me from him?'

The goshawk fluttered down. 'I have word from him.'

He dropped the letter, and the lady picked it up and read, smiling, flushing with joy.

'Lord William canna come. Your father would lie in wait and your brothers too, with sword and spear. But he kens you will find a way to come to him.'

'I'll come, I'll come. Fly back, my bonny bird, and bid my love brew the bridal ale and have the bridal cake baked. I'll be with him at the kirk where he has appointed the tryst. I'll be with him ere the ale has grown flat or the cake stale.'

The bird flew off. Lady Jean went to her father. 'Father, dear Father, I beg a boon.'

'What is it, my dear lass?' – her father spoke indulgently. He was ready to grant her almost anything – except the one desire of her heart, to marry her true love, Lord William.

'Only this: that if I die here in England, I may be taken over the Border to be buried in Scotland.'

Her father laughed. 'That I will grant. But you are not like to die, my bonny lass, with your lips and your cheeks so red and fresh, your eyes so bright.'

'And this too, my father dear. Let my shroud be sewn with silver bells all over. And when I am carried over the Border, let Mass be said at the first kirk we come to; at the second let all the bells be rung; and at the third let the bier be set down for a while.'

'Och, but you young lassies have many a strange fancy. I'll be dead and in my grave and Mass said for me long ere you come to that. But I promise you, my dear, what you ask.'

He laughed again, and Lady Jean laughed and went off to her bower and her own room. There she swallowed a sleeping draught and lay down. Sleep came upon her like the sleep of death.

They came, her sisters, then her father and brothers and her stepmother, to stand over her and try to rouse her. But there was no motion in her.

'We'll see if she be truly dead,' said her spiteful stepmother. 'Drop a bit of burning lead on her breast' – and that was done. Few could have borne such pain, but the brave lass lay utterly still, utterly silent.

'She is truly dead,' her father declared with a sigh, and he told them the promises he had given.

Her sisters made her shroud, at every stitch sewing on a silver bell. She was laid on her bier, and her brothers took it on their shoulders.

Up over the Border they carried her, into Scotland. At the first kirk they came to, Mass was said. At the second all the silver bells were rung. At the third kirk they set down the bier. And there stood a company of spearmen, silent, armed and ready. From among them came their chief, Lord William.

'Stand back and let me look upon my love,' he commanded, and they obeyed.

There she lay in her white shroud that was no whiter than

her face. But as her lover looked at her, she stirred, sat up and smiled.

'I have come, my love, as you bade me, and as I promised. Now give me a piece of bread to eat and red wine to drink, for I have fasted these three days for love of you.'

Source:
Sir Walter Scott, *The Minstrelsy of the Scottish Borders*

The Collectors

Allan Cunningham (1784–1842) was born in Keir, Dumfries-shire; he was educated at a dame school, and apprenticed stone-mason to an elder brother. He read all the books he could find, including Scott's poems. Like Hogg, whom he met and with whom he became friendly, he inherited a great deal from his mother, whose 'marked intellectual power was transmitted to her children' (*Dictionary of National Biography*). He wrote many poems, some in the traditional style and language, and novels. He also wrote for *Blackwood's Magazine* and in 1822 published *Traditional Tales of the English and Scottish Peasantry* in two volumes.

Sir George Douglas (1856–1935) was a Border Laird in Roxburghshire, a minor poet, a biographer – of James Hogg the Ettrick Shepherd – and essayist (*Diversions of a Country Gentleman*). He lectured on Scottish Literature in Glasgow University.

William Henderson was born on the other side of the Border, in Durham; he was a scholar and a man of letters. In 1861 he was invited to lecture to the Durham Athenaeum as their president, and chose the subject of folklore. He showed his script to 'the accomplished editor of *The Monthly Packet*' (Charlotte Yonge), who 'expressed a wish that the lecture should be turned into an article for the magazine.' This was done and the article was the nucleus for the volume *Notes on the Folklore of the Northern Counties of England and the Borders* (1866). Much of his material he had, as he acknowledged, from a young medical student called Wilkie who lived at Bowden, near Eildon Hall, and who contributed something to Scott for his *Minstrelsy of the Scottish Border*. Scott procured for him an appointment in India, where he died young – but by no means unfulfilled.

James Hogg (1770–1835) the 'Ettrick Shepherd' as he was called during his double life as shepherd and author, was born in Ettrick on the Borders. His father was a shepherd, a good man and devout, and his mother a woman of very special heritage and gifts; she was the daughter of Will o' Phaup, the subject of one of the stories told in this book, and from him and further forebears she inherited a deep knowledge of Border ballads and legends. These, she sternly told Walter Scott when he visited her, were 'made for singin' an' no' for readin'', and when printed in his *Minstrelsy of the Scottish Border* were 'neither richt spelt nor richt set doun'.

Hogg left school early and went to the herding. An avid reader, he listened to his mother's tales and kept them in his heart and imagination, and that was the making of him as poet and story-teller as well as collector.

He began to write and to publish poems and stories; he visited Edinburgh, was one of the Blackwood group with Lockhart and Wilson (Christopher North), and appears often in the latter's *Noctes Ambrosianae*. His selection of contributions to *Blackwood's Magazine* under the title *The Shepherd's Calendar* (1829) is the original source of some of the tales told in this book. As a shepherd he wrote *The Diseases of Sheep* which sold very well. It was while he was shepherd to Laidlaw of Blackhouse, whose son Will was secretary and companion to Scott, that he met that great Borderer, poet and collector, and took him to visit his formidable mother. He had his own sheep farm, latterly at Altrive in Selkirkshire, and so the double life continued until the end of his life. He wrote, besides much else, a memoir *The Domestic Manners and Private Life of Sir Walter Scott* (1834).

Sir Walter Scott (1771–1832), like Hogg, was very much more than a collector. He was a poet and novelist, laird, lawyer and Sheriff of Selkirk, living a complex life and himself a deep and complex character. He was born in Edinburgh, spent his early childhood on his grandfather's farm on the Borders, and was educated at Edinburgh High School and University. Having read law, he was admitted advocate at Parliament House. His father, a solicitor and Writer to the Signet, is portrayed, with young Scott himself, in *Redgauntlet*.

He began collecting poems and ballads in the Borders around 1800, and his *Minstrelsy of the Scottish Border* was published in 1802. In 1811–12 he moved to Abbotsford; in 1814 he published *Waverley*, first of the Waverley Novels. All his work, in poetry and prose, is full of traditional lore. He was both collector and creator.

John Mackay Wilson (1804–35), who collected the *Tales of the Borders*, was the son of a millwright. He served his apprenticeship as a printer and went for a time to London but came home to the Borders to become editor of the *Berwick Advertiser* and to gather his rich collection of *Tales*. He had a band of collaborators, of whom Alexander Leighton contributed the story of 'Helen of Kirkconnel' and Alexander Campbell that of 'The Monks of Dryburgh', while he himself contributed 'The Laidly Worm of Spindleston Heugh'.

Bibliography

The following sources have been used in the preparation of this book:

James Wood Brown: *Enquiry into the Life and Legend of Michael Scot* (1887)

Allan Cunningham: *Traditional Tales of the English and Scottish Peasantry* (1822; 1874)

Sir George Douglas: *Scottish Fairy and Folk Tales*, selected and edited by Sir George Douglas (1893)

William Henderson: *Notes on the Folklore of the Northern Counties of England and the Borders* (1866)

James Hogg: *The Ettrick Shepherd's Tales* (1 volume edition, 1874)

Dinah Maria Mulock (Mrs Craik): *Alice Learmont* (1852)

Sir Walter Scott: *Minstrelsy of the Scottish Border* (1802; in 4 volumes, edited by T. Henderson, 1902)

John Mackay Wilson: *Tales of the Borders* (10 volumes, edited by Alexander Leighton, 1888)

The following modern editions are listed for further reading:

Scottish Fairy and Folk Tales, selected and edited by Sir George Douglas (contains Wood Brown, Cunningham, Henderson and Hogg), EP Publishing (1977)

James Hogg: *Selected Stories and Sketches*, edited by Douglas Mack,
   Scottish Academic Press (1982)
Sir Walter Scott: *The Minstrelsy of the Scottish Border*, edited by
   Alfred Noyes, Mercat Press, James Thin (1979)